Memoir

Of a

Children's

Convalescent Home

1947-49.

By

Eleanor Eadie

And

Stuart Rushworth.

(For Ruth.)

Chapter 1.

I leant my head back on the upholstered seat of the railway carriage and listened to the rhythmical clickety-clack of the train steaming its way to Manchester. Gazing out of the window I saw that we had left behind all signs of life, there was nothing but moorland as far as the eye could see. The October sky was overcast, lending the barren landscape an ominous and dramatic appearance that in fact matched my mood, for I was fearful of the unknown and no matter how I tried I could not conjure up any optimistic thoughts to pierce my darkness.

Seated opposite me was my escort who was to take me to a hospital in Cheshire. He looked to be around forty years of age, was rather thin with sunken cheeks and thinning hair and he was reading a newspaper.

The train pulled up at a station and a man and his wife entered our compartment and my escort looked up briefly and nodded to them then returned to his paper. The couple made themselves comfortable.

I studied the lady, she looked to be in her forties too but was fashionably dressed with a luxurious warm scarf draped around her shoulders. The hat she wore was perched on the top of her head and slanted towards her forehead, I had seen my mam looking longingly at this style of hat in the shops. I found myself trying very hard to imagine that it was my mam sitting there, for I had a great need to fill the chasm left behind left after our tearful goodbyes at the station that morning. I closed my eyes in an attempt visualise Mam with that hat on her head, her eyes sparkling with happiness, but the illusion was denied me. I blinked back my tears as I recalled standing on the platform of Sowerby Bridge Station earlier that day saying goodbye to her. My mother had cried and I had grasped her hand and had begged to be taken home. She had tearfully replied that I could not be. I buried my face in her coat and had let out a high pitched terrified scream. I could see her face in my mind's eye as she tearfully waved. As the train slowly pulled out of the station I had felt alone and abandoned.

Rain began to spit and splat on the window , and my eyes returned to my escort, His newspaper was now in his lap, held loosely with one hand. His head was laid back. His eyes were closed and his mouth was open and from which I detected an almost inaudible snore.

I began to look around the carriage. On the wall facing me was a colourful holiday poster showing a golden beach and a pretty smiling girl holding a beach ball and with happy families in the background. Behind the poster was the faded old notice of what to do in the event of an air raid. I looked through the window again with thoughts of how frightening it must have been to sit in this very carriage during an air raid.

The gentle putt-putt snore was still escaping from my escort so I reached over and shook his arm, fearing that we might miss our stop. He opened his eyes, looked around and said:

"We are not ther' yet, Miss," he said, whilst looking towards our fellow passengers. "If yer would sit quietly please."

I too shut my eyes.

I remembered an evening not so long before when my mam had been warming her legs against the heat of the coal fire, a habit that had caused her skin to become mottled. She would regularly wring her hands and complain that we had no money spare since Dad's illness and saying how relieved she would be when the money they had borrowed was paid back. My dad would sit in our corner shop and count the points he had cut out of the customers' ration books during the day

It was no shame to be short of money, after all many others had been discharged from the forces during the war on medical grounds. Maybe one day he would be able to throw his crutches into the dustbin and Mam could be a housewife again. Perhaps he could go back to his skilled job in the mill and we could once again live in a nice house, like the semi-detached house we had lived in before the onset of the war.

Our shop was a small grocery store and we lived in accommodation over the shop. The property was old and damp and although the landlord was happy to collect the rent he was stone deaf when repairs were needed. When dry rot caused a hole in the floorboards in the front bedroom Mam placed the draw-tin that we used to draw the fire over the decay and simply hoped for the best.

The back bedroom was where my sister and I slept but which had flourishing fungi on the walls. Mam tried distempering the walls but within days the fungus was back. So when I developed a cough Mam claimed it was the spores from the fungus getting into my lungs and she blamed the landlord.

My five year old sister and I spent more time in our neighbour's house than our own. Mam and Dad paid them to look after us when they had long hours to work in the shop. Mam used to get so tired. Dad did his best but most of the work such as serving and cleaning fell on Mam's shoulders, whilst Dad did the bookkeeping and kept a check on the stock. Our neighbours had four children of their own and they were glad of the extra money we paid for their care.

I had begun to have frequent periods of feeling unwell and was unable to attend school. My absences were a welcome break from the psychological bullying I received from some of my classmates. I had gained the nickname 'Wheezie-Anna' due to my constant coughing and wheezing. The ribbing upset me and I had become a loner with very few friends. I hated school and everyone in it.

The train was slowing down and my escort was now wide awake and I could hear the station guard shouting *"Manchester!"*

I stiffly stood up and stepped down onto the platform. My escort grabbed my hand and we headed for a freshment room. The thin air in the station was heavy with smoke and piercing noises hit my ears from every direction: There was the hiss of the steam, the chuff of the engines, the slamming of doors and whistles blowing.Also watched people rushing hither and thither in business suits or weekday clothes. Many were standing with luggage whilst others were men in uniform who were jumping off trains and swinging their kit bags.

I asked my escort if we were in Cheshire yet.

"Good grief no," he replied. "We 'ave to catch another train, Miss, that would be to Liverpool yet, and a busan' all," he said."

I was next seated on the next train bound for Livrpool, feeling replenished after a sandwich and a hot drink. This was a corridor train and passengers were walking by and I watched a group of young sailors enter our compartment. They we in high spirits and chattering noisily about going home.

I listened, though not so much to what they had to say but instead to how they said it. It was the Liverpool, or Scouse, accent I was hearing, an accent I was going to hear for my whole stay in the hospital.

I began to tired so I closed my eyes again.

The day the letter had arrived from The Education Authority was news of a threat of court action unless proof of a valid reason was received for my many days absent from school. Mam had been angry and upset but her anger had turned to concern when a medical examination revealed how poorly I was. Her long hours in the shop had made her oblivious to my slow but steady weight loss, and she had simply dosed me with herbal remedies.

The outcome of it all was that I was to be placed in a hospital on The Wirral where the air was fresh and pure. Mam was not at all happy about this.

"It will not be easy to visit - going such a distance in one day," she said.

This has caused me to wonder where exactly The Wirral was.

Many dozings and recollections later my escort made ready.

"Act lively, Miss - we are nearly in Liverpool," he said.

My sailor travel companions were now talking nineteen to the dozen, guffawing and joking with each other. How I envied them having each other, their not being alone like me. I realised then and for the first time in my life that I was truly loved.

I stepped out of the carriage and into another crowd in another city and we walked swiftly past the engine, and what a brute it looked close up, with steam spitting and smoke pluming each time the engine puffed. I felt like I was standing next to a dragon. As if that monster had read my thoughts it sent out a jet of steam from between its wheels onto the platform. The shrieking hissing noise made us both jump, my escort and I began laughing, and my day at that moment seemed not to be so bad after all.

Next there was a walk through tremendous city through fayres but with the crowd so often blocking my view. Our haste brought us to a bus station and after another encounter with crowds wer sped hence. Our bus passed houses, all clean and bright, their brickwork a bright russet. I thought of the houses back in the Pennine village where I lived that was set deep in the heart of the woollen industry in the West Riding of Yorkshire. There blackened mills dominated the landscape while black chimney stacks emitted sulphurous fumes day and night.

Even the trees looked downcast and dirty.

I noticed the people we passed and they too were different from people at home, for not one single man was wearing clogs, hobnail boots or an overall smeared with grease. There were no women with hair and clothes with woolly strands clinging to them from working in the weaving sheds. Here women were cleanly attired with no turbaned headscarves wrapped about their heads.

Oh how my mam would have loved living here!

I thought about her on her hands and knees scrubbing our doorstep every week - a futile task, since within hours the doorstep was dirty again.

Next I saw a great expanse of water.

"That is th' River Dee," my escort said knowledgeably, "and that will be Wales on that far bank, and if yer look yer'll see those blurry shapes there, well they are the Welsh mountains."

The line of hazy purple shapes were there on the horizon, like it was a distant fog. Back home we had horrible fogs,' when the smoke got trapped in it and when you could not see your hand before your face. People walked about with handkerchiefs across their mouths to avoid breathing in the poisonous air. When the fog and smoke combined like that the buses were called in, so that people had to walk to work, regardless of the distance.

We stepped off the bus into that clear fresh day and as we walked down the street and I breathed the air my mam had said would make me better. It was a pure soft air with a hint of the smell of burning leaves. There was no choking stench of ammonia from the mills. It was clean and quite beautiful place.

Then as we walked an imposing building came into view amd when when we stood before its gates my escort placed a reassuring hand upon my shoulder. He smiled:

"We 'ave arrived at yer 'ospital," he said with tone of accomplishment.

My first sight of the hospital acted like a lightning bolt. I felt my pulse quickening and while my hands became clammy and sweaty. Weariness was overtaken by fear as I gazed disbelievingly at the large and wide two-storey building with its ornamental spire and heavy gables. I had mentally pictured the hospital as being about the size of my small school, but this building was unfathomable and towered and gaunt. The afternoon westerly sun illuminated the facade, making the brickwork glint. I could not discover how far back the building went.

The roof comprised of numerous tall chimneys, a dome, and two spires. One tower had a flagpole on the top, while its neighbour had a weather vane. There were a great many windows, both mullioned and bayed, and all of them looked secretive and black. One exception was a strange looking room extending on the right side of the building that had only a low wall and a gap above it and wire-netting like a cage. That rather 'cave-like' place was furnished with rows of neatly made beds..

The hospital besides its looming exterior was set in extensive grounds with neat lawns, flowerbeds and shrubberies, enclosed by a perimeter wall that was topped with wrought iron railings and gates. A glass-fronted case containing information about the hospital and a collection box for donations was there, where a gravel drive began and swept around to an imposing front door.

The sun slid behind a cloud and I began to imagine that the windows were sightless eyes staring blackly at all that had gone before for me, and that seemed knowledgeable also of what was to come.

The illusion caused me to shiver, at which point the escort took my hand, opened one of the gates and we walked along to where he pressed a brass doorbell.

Thereafter we stood waiting like we should never enter and perhaps turn and simply go home, go home no matter how dirty and smoky it was.

Chapter 2.

A nurse ushered us into an entrance lobby with a desk and some chairs. She asked us to take a seat and then settled herself at a desk and began filling in a form.

"Date of birth?" she asked, to which gave my details meekly.

Smiling reassuringly at me the form-filling continued

I noticed her accent was the same as the sailors who had shared our railways carriage.

Next she talked to my escort, but I wasn't listening, for I was looking about the room.

There was a large picture of the hospital on one wall whilst on another there was an oil painting of a dour-looking elderly woman seated stiffly in a wooden chair with her hands crossed on her lap. By her side was a wicker table on which there was an open book and where also a pen and an inkwell rested.

I hoped that I would not be meeting the likes of her in here, for she looked rather strict with piercing eyes and a cruel mouth.

I looked back at the nurse, who was once again talking to me.

"You will be in Fortitude Ward, and the Sister is Sister Devereaux who is in overall charge, and you will be meeting her soon."

She smiled again.

"A doctor will decide what treatment you are to receive, but to do that he will have to examine you, Eleanor."

I nodded then noticed my escort was preparing to leave.

He knelt down beside me.

"I hope yer'll be feeling better very soon, Miss," he said. Then standing and turning and waving to both of us, he was gone.

I felt bereft without him.

The nurse smiled kindly at me.

"You have nothing at all to worry about," she said, and she led me from the lobby and into one of many a corridors. We turned right and passed numerous closed doors while the floor was parquet tile and highly polished. I detected the faint aroma of floor polish, but which was this was overpowered by a pervading insistent smell, which I later learned was a disinfectant called carbolic.

There were all sorts of sounds both around me and in the distance. I could hear muffled voices behind closed doors. I heard a distant clanging noise as if someone was wheeling something heavy, and also the footsteps of people walking elsewhere. At regular intervals there were fire doors that each had a fire extinguisher. In addition there were hoses coiled on reels in glass faced cabinets marked with the caption:

Break in the Event of Fire

At one place a nurse came out of a room followed by a whoosh of warm air that smelled of sticking plasters and the two nurses exchanged pleasantries in the same lilting Liverpool accent.They talked about the cinema and then such things that only their profession might know.

Then the two friends bade each other goodbye and my nurse led me along the corridor once more. As she went she plied me with reassuring words I came to understand that with her interest in Hollywood stars and her casual manner that the nurses were just like ordinary people back home. They had chatted just like my mother talked to our next door neighbour. I found this very comforting.

Nurses were everywhere. Nurses were walking up and down the corridor and in and out of doors. A doctor in a white coat with a stethoscope about his neck walked briskly by. A nurse passed by pushing a sickly boy in a wheelchair.

Then when we passed a door that was slightly ajar I heard the terrified shriek of a child, followed by the calming voice of a nurse.

"No now, you must hold still."

This filled me with trepidation again so that I pulled on the nurse's hand, trying to remove my fingers from her grip. She paused and calmed me, after which I reluctantly walked on.

This had all begun to feel like I should be Alice on her journey through Wonderland. The front door through which I had entered was lost to me forever, just as her rabbit-hole had been. I was bewildered by the corridors where doors gave a the briefest glimpses of mysterious rooms.

We passed through another fire door and there was a cleaning lady with an electric floor polisher buffing the parquet tiles and once we were away from the noise my nurse apple to me.

"This is the section of the hospital where you will be," she said. "You will be shown around so that you can get your bearings," she added.

I grasped her hand even tighter, for all around me was the clamour of the staff busy with their daily work, whilst not a single child's voice was audible to me.

I wondered where all the patients were.

We waited and then through a door at the far end of the corridor there stepped a nurse. She walked briskly towards us, her starched uniform swishing as she moved. She greeted me, and then peered down through thick lens spectacles.

"I am Nurse Mollett, " she said stooping to smile at me.

Then Nurse Mollett thanked the other nurse for escorting me.

"I am sorry I was late, " she said to her, "I've been chasing myself around; God help me if Sister Devereaux finds out," she said, at which the nurses exchanged alarmed faces.

Whilst they talked I was observing Nurse Mollett. She suffered from acne on her face, especially her cheeks and chin, and also she had blemishes from spots that had healed. I wondered if she felt self-conscious like me. Her uniform consisted of a short sleeved light blue starched dress, some white arm-bands with frilly edges were worn to draw her sleeves. As well as these her a small collar protruded about her neck, while on her head she wore a small white cap that partly covered her covering frizzy brown hair. A heavily starched white apron had straps that crossed on her back, and finally she wore black stockings and black shoes.

The two nurses glanced at their tab watches and the nurse that was leaving made mention of her own superior, who was a SIster Rumbold.

That nurse then gave me a hug and then walked back down the corridor and then through the fire doors, which closed noisily behind her.

Nurse Mollett led me along a t a quickened pace, as if this Sister Devereaux was marching after us and I imagined a great battle-axe of a woman as austere as the figure in the oil painting. in the reception room.

Therefore in our own ways we might have been both afraid as our journey through the noisy corridors continued, each step being a step nearer to the one we both feared.

Chapter 3.

The events which took place over the next hour evoked many distressing emotions, and I felt absolutely wretched, for I had exchanged the love and cosiness of my family for the demands of this totally alien place.

We were joined by another nurse, who turned out to be an even busier one.

I was taken to a bathroom and saw the shiny white bathtub, and the walls that were tiled right up to the ceiling.

We did not have a bathroom back home, for hung on our kitchen wall was a tin bath that Mam filled with hot water from the clothes boiler. We all had to bathe in the same water, and then the bath had to be emptied using a ladling can.

The procedure, however, was far preferable to this modern clinical room where the nurse bathed me in a disinfectant bath, rubbing my skin with a rough flannel. She then washed my hair, not even attempting to prevent the soapy water from stinging my eyes.

My mam had washed and set my hair that morning, and it distressed me even further to know her efforts had been in vain.

My head was then treated for the prevention of head lice. My mam would have been horrified, because she always kept my head so clean.

The nurse took me out of the bath and wrapped me in a towel, then she told me to sit on a wooden stool.

I could hear the snick, snick, snick of scissors as huge clumps of wet hair began to fall into my lap or onto the floor. She was not trimming strands of hair like Mam did, but instead hacking it off.

The sight of all that hair falling around me struck me dumb. I could not control the tears that flowed and dripped off the end of my nose.

Next I felt clippers running up the back of my head. The nurse, on seeing my tears, paused to talk to me.

"Long hair saps the strength of the body," she said with assuredness. "Surely you do not want to be weak?" she added. "You want to get better and go home again?

I stood with my eyes lowered while the nurse dressed me in a cotton gown.

I was next taken to a waiting-room.

"A doctor will see you shortly," the nurse said quickly and left.

I was to sit on one of the seats and wait.

From that moment on terror of the unknown gripped me like a vice. I sat limply, staring at the closed door that was facing me.

The door opened and another nurse said I was now to go into the examination room and once there a doctor in a white coat made the examination, speaking only to instruct me. I silently obeyed whilst finding it difficult to control my nervous trembling.

When the examination was over I was issued with a set of winter clothing consisting of a vest; knickers; a liberty bodice; a navy blue serge skirt with a cotton bodice top; a navy blue jumper, a pair of grey knee length socks and finally a pinafore. The pinafore was sax blue and was almost like a dress, for it had a yoke and at the back it was open while there was deep frill around the edges of the armholes. To wear the pinafore I had to pull it over my head like a frock. Then after receiving these there were also things to carry, including a long-sleeved fleecy nightdress, a handkerchief that was no more than a scrap of white cotton material, frayed from constant laundering. I was to wear my own slippers and shoes, the slippers and socks being the only required items I had carried. The outdoor clothing consisted of a navy blue winter coat and a matching beret. Lastly I was issued with a comb and a facecloth, both having a name-tag attached to it.

I was to use my own toothbrush and toothpaste.

I was then shown to a cloakroom and upon entering the cloakroom I froze, since the last time I had looked in a mirror I had seen a thin pale-faced girl with brown eyes and shoulder length straight brown hair.

The image that I knew had been replaced by a girl with a blotchy face, with eyes red and swollen from crying, and whose hair looked like a pudding basin had been placed on the top of her head as a prelude to that severe cutting.

My appearance shocked me.

I felt ugly.

Next I was shown Fortitude Ward, where I was to sleep. I was surprised to find that the ward had only three solid walls; the fourth wall was about three feet high, above which was stretched wire netting. It was the 'cave' I had seen from my view of the building outside.

Nurse Mollett, who returned as the only person I seemed to properly know, had me stand beside my bed.

"Eleanor, this is what is called an 'Open Air Ward,'" she said. "It is extremely beneficial for patients who have chest-related illnesses, such as yourself."

Then she touched my shoulder.

"We are going to make you well again."

The coldness of the ward was unbelievable, for the changing weather was sending raindrops through the wire netting and it spit and spatted on my face and on the beds and on the bare concrete floor.

Daylight was dwindling and the overhead electric lights were dim, giving the room a bleak and depressing mood.

I seriously doubted Nurse Mollett's words, for how could sleeping in so exposed a place possibly make me any better? Surely I should catch pneumonia or worse!

There were three rows of beds and I had been given a bed on the middle row next to the wall that divided our ward from Patience Ward to the right I felt grateful that I did not have a bed either side of me, for at least I would be able to turn away and not have to look at the girl to my right side. I had been allocated a locker that was beside my bed and that should contain my few possessions.

Upon my arrival I had been like Alice in Wonderland, but now I felt I had lapsed into the grim world of Oliver Twist, though Oliver's bed had offered more comfort than this one.

No doubt even worse was to come in the form of Sister Devereaux, whom I did not want to meet. I so desperately wanted to go home, but I knew there was no escape from this nightmare world that I had found myself trapped in.

Lastly I was taken to a dining room.

It was a pleasant room. It had a large imposing Victorian fireplace on the right wall that had a black leaded fire grate. A huge coal fire was blazing and sending out heat, so that with these extremes of hot and cold I felt like Alice again. The hearth tiles were dark green and above the tall mantelshelf was a large Victorian mirror mottled with age. Gleaming brass ornaments rested on the mantelshelf and while a brass fender enclosed the hearth. The whole fireplace was surrounded by a mesh fireguard with a brass trim and next to the fireplace stood a shiny brass coal scuttle full of fuel. To right of the hearth stood an upright piano and while wicker chairs that had seen better days were set either side of the fire, Their only use was as storage place for toys. Both chairs seemed overburdened with the weight of piles of dollies, teddies and other playthings.

Some windows opposite faced onto the side gardens abd the light from there showed the solid benches that were set to every extent of the walls. Immediately to my right, meaning the nearside wall was glazed in into upper extent so that on tip toe I should have been able to look down into Fortitude Ward, which through its removed flooring was set deeper.

Set flush to the unglazed walls were ornately carved benches in the style of church pews. The wood was smooth and rather elegant from constantly being sat upon. In contrast the many many trestle tables that stood in front of these were plain deal, neither painted nor stained. Their surfaces were worn and between each table there was a gap for children to reach the benches. Apart from these and in the very centre of the room and set apart from all other things was a desk and a chair.

Nurse Mollett and I turned when there suddenly entered from behind us an overweight woman with a sad-looking face who was wearing a cook's smock and cap and she was towing a trolley behind her.

Then Nurse Mollett had me sit down at one of the trestle tables and after this the cook placed before me a stew served on an aluminium dish, together with a knife and fork. An aluminium mug, badly misshapen from frequent use, was filled with tea from an urn on the trolley.

The cook then then went on her way dragging the trolley behind her.

I had always been accustomed to eating off earthenware, and the meal before me looked unappetizing against the metal. I picked my knife and fork, hesitated, and then placed then placed my utensils down on the table again, after which I sat in grim silence.

Nurse Mollett sat down in front of me and she picked up the fork and she tried to feed me like a baby.

I gritted my teeth defiantly.

She watched me with some caution.

"To refuse to eat is not an option here," she warned before she sat back. "We shall sit here until midnight until you have eaten," she said.

I considered her words and decided to choose the easy option, so taking the fork from her hand I began to eat. Fear had robbed me of my appetite, and yet I dared not disobey, and with concentrated effort I cleared the plate as I was required to.

Nurse Mollett smiled.

"You have been a good girl," she said roundly, "i can see you are going to fit in well in this hospital."

I doubted this very much.

Next sounds of children's voices reached my ears from down the corridor and the sounds were getting louder.

Nurse Mollett looked towards the door.

"Those will be the patients who have just returned from their afternoon walk," she said, before listening. "They are queuing for the toilets right now," she said, "then they will bathing or showering."

She stood up.

"You remain where you are and Sister Devereaux will be meeting with you soon," she said.

Nurse Mollett then seated herself at the desk and took care of documents that were there. A few moments later the dining room door opened and a shorter and slimmer nurse entered and after some discussion she took over from Nurse Mollett and continued with the paperwork as Nurse Mollett left.

The space of the dining room seemed to increase and I came to watch the dining room door with an increasing fixedness.

I began to consider how I should conduct myself. Nurse Mollett had suggested Sister was very experienced and a perfectionist. Therefore in order to impress Sister Devereaux I should project a perfect image.

My Grandma's words of wisdom came to mind.

'A child should speak only when spoken to.'

Therefore I decided that I would not speak first. Then also I should remember to say please and thank you.

The door opened suddenly and a nurse wearing blue hurried in with a heavy step, her starched uniform rustling as she walked. She spoke with the young nurse at the desk who immediately left the room.

This new rather resolute nurse opened a desk drawer and took out a file and began reading.

My interest switched back to the door. There was a spring at the top of the door that made it close automatically each time it was opened. I had been observing the doorknob and noticed that it was rather slack fitting, so that it would wobble when turned.

I fixed my eyes on it.

The knob wobbled and I clenched my fists to steady my nerves as it turned and the door opened. It was the lady in the cook's smock and cap who entered and collected the dirty plate and cup. She smiled at me before walking back through the door.

My gaze became fixed on the doorknob again as I readied myself.

How should I present myself perfectly to Sister Devereaux?

My mam often chastised me for not being bold and assertive, so was this an imperfection? I had always been a loner, preferring my own company to that of others, so was this too a fault?

I began to run over the main points. Well mannered, speak only when spoken to. Have a confident air.

Yet again the door opened but the small nurse had returned. The two nurses spoke and then taller nurse left the room.

Dusk was falling outside and I noticed a lamplighter with his long pole lighting up the gas streetlamps beyond the hospital railings outside. However I afforded him only a cursory glance, my gaze returning to the door. The noise of the patients was growing louder.

The duty nurse checked her watch and she also made ready to leave. She walked across the room and left.

Then gradually I heard the high-spirited laughter and chatter in the corridor was hushed and I knew that Sister Deveraux had arrived.

The knob moved and turned and then the door opened and I sighed a sigh of relief when it was only the duty nurse returning.

I was now beginning to wish that Sister Devereaux had walked through the door, for the anticipation of her arrival was becoming more and more stressful.

The duty nurse then returned to her desk and then glancing across at me she spoke.

"Come here, child!"

Her voice startled me and I visibly jumped, which caused a slight smile to show and then vanish.

She beckoned me with the forefinger of her right hand and repeated.

"Come here!"

I rose, and with my eyes darting between her and the doorknob, I walked across to the desk.

I noticed no how blue her eyes were. Her long brown shiny hair was pinned up beneath her cap. Her hands that rested on a blotting pad on the desk, were small with long fingers and had neatly trimmed fingernails. She was petite, having no size to her.

Her dress was a darker blue than those of the other nurses. She had a white collar with detachable starched white cuffs at the wrists. Her white apron had no straps, and instead it was fastened at the front of her dress with two ornate safety pins. Her cap was slightly different too, forit had a frill around its edges.

She spoke yet again in a very clear and refined and cultured English accent of a kind that I had only heard on the radio in those days.

"Hello Eleanor. I am Sister Devereaux."

I felt like an explosion had taken place inside my head and all my preparations were in tatters.

I found myself unable to utter a single word. Instead I swallowed as my throat tightened and I lowered my eyes.

Sister Devereaux continued.

"You are to refer to me as Sister when addressing me, and please look at me when I am speaking to you."

I could not look up, for I knew that the tears were not very far away.

I remained stiff and mute with my downcast eyes.

She stood and reached out her hand and placing her fingers under my chin she forcibly made me look at her, while she in her turn looked at me with clear blue eyes.

I began to cry.

She was about to speak again when the door opened and Nurse Mollett entered and hurried over to the desk.

Sister's attention was now fixed on the nurse, and indeed I too was looking at her.

Nurse Mollette asked Sister Deveraux what action should be taken regarding a child in a ward called 'Courtesy Ward.'

Nurse Mollett fell silent, waiting for a reply.

When Sister Devereaux's reply came she reminded me of an angry snake.

"Why are you asking me this question?" she snapped and with anger burning in her eyes.

I saw nurse Mollett recoil from the acid delivery, but she quickly recovered her composure and replied.

"Because you asked me to monitor the child, Sister."

"Indeed I did," Sister Devereaux said, "but that does not mean you had to walk the full length of the corridor to find me when Staff Nurse Briggs was surely closer to hand!"

Sister Devereaux paused to let her words sink in and then she continued with that biting conciseness.

"Just for once, Mollett, can you use a little common sense? Have you got a brain inside that head of yours?"

Nurse Mollett stood silent.

"Well? Good grief nurse! Go and find Staff Nurse Briggs!"

Then as an afterthought, with her blue eyes steely with annoyance, she added:

"I don't want any further interruptions of this nature when I am otherwise engaged. Understood!"

I could not recall ever having encountered such a rude, arrogant person in my life, and I felt so sorry for Nurse Mollett, who had meekly listened to the tirade, and then apologised and then quickly left the room. I was amazed that Nurse Mollett had not cowered or even burst into tears and that indeed she did not seem unduly upset.

Sister Devereaux's attention now returned to me, and the remnants of the icy coldness remained in her eyes. I had a sinking feeling in my stomach and once again I lowered my eyes. A feeling of hatred for this horrid little woman was fast beginning to develop, together with a dread of what lay ahead.

"Look at me!" she ordered once again and reaching out she forcibly raised my face.

I reluctantly looked at her, as scalding tears began to cloud my vision and stream down my cheeks.

In times past when I was in distress my mother would comforted me with tender words of endearment. I was to receive no such comfort from Sister Deverreaux. Instead she assumed a stern expression and pointing she said sharply:

"Stop those tears immediately!"

I choked on the next sob that was rising in my breast.

"I said STOP!" she repeated.

Never in my whole life had I been spoken to like this. A surge of anger began to rise within me. I detested this thin-faced little woman, and I found myself comparing her to the wicked witches in the land of fairytales.

How I began to loathe her.

She continued.

"I would expect this behaviour from a five year old, but I do not expect it from a ten year old, and I demand that you look at me when I am speaking to you and answer any questions I may ask you."

Anger is a powerful emotion, more potent than fear, and it rapidly checked my tears.

I raised my chin and looked at her defiantly, not even trying to disguise my contempt.

My reaction must have been what she was seeking, for her features softened slightly and the ghost of a smile touched her lips.

She seated herself. removed her hands from the desk and leaned back in her chair and then was silently observing me from the top of my head down to my feet.

"We are all here to make you better, but we cannot do this alone. We need your cooperation," she said. "I want to see a brave little girl, ready and willing to climb all obstacles, not a cry-baby. Do you feel you are capable of this, or am I to be disappointed?"

I remained silent.

Then raising an eyebrow she waited.

"Well?" she asked,

I cleared my throat.

"Yes, Sister Devereaux, I will try."

"You will try what?"

"To be brave, Sister."

"Good!" she said." I want you to constantly bear in mind that all of my staff are your friends and not enemies. If you feel the need to talk, or have any queries, we will be only too pleased to listen. Have you any questions?"

"Yes. When can I go home?"

"Medicals are carried out every twelve weeks. The decision as to when you are deemed fit for discharge will be a doctor's, not mine."

She sat straight, placing her small hands once again on the blotter.

"I expect you to conduct yourself in a sociably acceptable manner whilst under my care. Failure to do so will result in loss of privileges, understood?"

"Yes, Sister Deveraux."

Then she motioned towards the benches and tables.

"The girls will now take their places in this dining room for their teatime meal. I will introduce you briefly, and then after you will retire immediately to bed, for you have had a taxing day. Come and stand at the side of me please," she said, so that I went along at a start.

She pointed her finger to where I should position myself.

When I had obeyed she walked over to the door and gave permission for a line of girls who had been queueing in the corridor to enter the dining-room.

I watched as in order of height the girls came through that door. They approached the end of a bench and then a smaller number walked along its length its length to their place.

"Be seated," ordered Sister.

They obeyed.

All eyed were then on me and I felt extremely uncomfortable.

Then Sisier Devereaux address them.

"This is Eleanor Eadie, a new patient whom I want you all to make welcome," she said.

Then all the girls chanted in unison.

"Hello Eleanor."

Nurse Moffett had returned and she took my hand and lead me out of the dining room, for which I was very grateful. She took me first to Patience Ward, which was next to Fortitude Ward.

Nurse Moffett helped me undress and put on my nightgown. I was then taken into Fortitude Ward and tucked up in bed.

Never in my whole life had I been so grateful to climb into bed, and even though a cold night wind was blowing across the ward this felt like a sanctuary.

To either side of Fortitude Ward were windows to lighted rooms.

Immediately to my left I could see the upper walls and the ceiling of Patience Ward and to my right I could see the same in the dining room. I could hear the clatter of plates and cups and the chatter of children's voices and I felt so glad that I was not still in there.

I must have dropped off to sleep because the next thing I knew the door of Fortitude Ward was opened and children poured through in their nightgowns and slipped quickly into their beds. The ward was a babble of conversations.

A girl in the bed next to mine asked me a question - I froze. I did not answer, and she thankfully did not persist, so I lay as quietly as I could, hoping that if I did not move I might become invisible.

After about half an hour the lights in the ward were turned off and all was quiet apart from nurses that were singing what might have been hymns in the dining room while the piano played.

I lay awake thinking of home. I wanted my mother. The friendly aroma of home had been replaced by carbolic and floor polish.

I began to miss the little things: The tick of the clock in my bedroom; the soft click when my mother closed the bedroom door after saying goodnight. I could no longer hear the ringing of the trains passing through my village, or the muffled sound of the radio that my parents listened to downstairs, which was often such a comforting sound.

At this point my emotions got the better of me and I began to silently weep, and the tears ran down down my cheeks. Then all of a sudden a warm hand was pressed into mine and a soft nurse's voice asked me what was the matter.

"I want to go home," I sobbed.

The nurse came close.

"You can go home in the morning," she said.

Those words were a balm to my troubled spirit, and I fell almost immediately into drowsiness and then sleep.

Chapter 4.

At 6.30 the following morning I was awakened by the clanking of enamel bowls being placed by the beds. A dark lethargy dulled my senses. I could not at first remember where I was until a nurse came to mt bed, loosened my bedclothes and told me to cough and spit into the bowl until she told me to stop.

I buried my face in the pillow and refused.

The nurse tried reasoning with me, but I would not heed her until I heard her say that she would have to fetch Sister if I refused to cough. I assumed she was referring to Sister Devereaux, and decided that I would rather cough than face her once again. I coughed and spit into the bowl until the said I had done well and that I could lie down in my bed again.

It felt good to slither down between the sheets, for the cold morning air had nipped at my shoulders, neck and arms, and leaning over the bed had caused the blood to surge to my head.

"Hello Eleanor," said a voice that sounded less coarse than my flat Yorkshire dialect. It was girl who had asked me a question the evening before and despite my shyness I looked through my fingers in that person's direction and saw it was a girl in the bed next to mine.

Then without pausing even to see what she looked like I quickly turned my back to her and buried my face in my pillow.

What was the point of replying when I was going home today? Then with a new realisation tears welled up at the thought of my release.

The girl beside me persisted.

"I heard Sister Kilshaw telling you that you could home," the voice said regardless of my ignoring her.

Then I heard her sit up in her bed.

"I am afraid she says that to all new girls to get them to sleep. She told me the same when I first came here."

The girl did not speak again. Only the babble of the girls talking to each other in the ward met my ears.

I remained hidden.

So the voice last night had belonged to someone called Sister Kilshaw, and she had lied to me.

I felt trapped.

I recalled once seeing in a book a picture of an insect trapped in a web. This whole building with its dark windows, long corridors and countless mysterious doors had swallowed me whole. I was entombed within it, just like the insect in the web, with no means of escaping.

"I am Christine," said the girl, whom I still refused to face or answer.

"Sister Kilshaw is the night sister and she is ever so nice, and she never gets cross with any of us. She only tells the lie to help us," Christine said.

I listened as she explained some more.

"My best friend slept in your bed, but she has gone home now and I really miss her. You see friends are allowed to sleep side by side," she said.

Then she paused.

"I am ten years old and I come from Berkshire," she said, "which is rather a long way south of here."

Christine paused.

"But my mummy and my daddy come to visit me, they never miss," she said.

At this I quickly turned to stare at her, for her for her mentioning visitors caught my interest.

Christine was a plain girl just as I was.

She smiled.

"Visitors are allowed here for one hour on every third Saturday," she said.

Then she peered down at the concrete floor as if something had caught her attention.

"You must never leave your slippers there or there will be bugs and spiders in them. You must always put your slippers in your locker just as I did."

I shook my slippers and there were indeed creepy crawlies spilling out.

I squirmed.

Christine nodded.

"It is one of the hazards of sleeping outdoors," Christine said dolefully.

Then she spent some time banging my slippers on the concrete floor until she was sure they were de-bugged.

"Thank you," I managed to say, before pushing my slippers down in my bed to make sure nothing else crept into them.

"We will be getting up soon," she said. "I will show you everything, everything you need to know. All you have to do is copy whatever I do."

Then she paused.

"You have to keep your hand on your hankie, that is very important, because there are thieves about."

I looked at her with disbelief.

Christine laughed.

"You have so much to learn, if if you don't then I expect you will find out the hard way."

She lapsed into silence then, and to my surprise I found myself wanting her to continue talking to me. I tried to think of something to say but I could not and remained mute.

It was a great relief when Christine eventually spoke again.

"The day-shift are coming on duty. She said."

I looked through the corridor windows and saw some young women walking by.

"They work shifts but you don't always know who is on duty," Christine said.

"I know Nurse Mollett," I said with a moment of realisation, "she is nice."

"They are all nice," Christine replied, "especially Nurse Owens who has a Welsh accent. Every patient likes her, and the girls wish they looked like her too. She is always talking about her boyfriends."

I then felt brave enough to ask Christine what our routine was.

"Nothing much happens. Basically it is boring," she said. "Today is like yesterday and tomorrow will be like today, except for Sundays; they are - awful."

We continued talking and conversation came easy for me, something I had rarely experienced outside the confines of my own home. The only exception had been when we had an evacuee staying with us during the war. She had been a part of our family. I had cried when she went home. Now it seemed I had a second friend that I really liked, and what is more, which I could hardly believe, she liked me too.

New patients were watched over carefully by the nursing staff and given assistance whenever necessary, but in certain cases patients who knew the routine well were all too willing to take new girls under their wing and show them what to do. When this occurred nursing staff rarely interfered. Christine had already decided that she was going to look after me, and she told me as much before reminding me that all I had to do was copy her.

At 7.00am we arose and we put on our slippers and made our way to the toilets.

We queued up at the washroom and toilet doors and entered four at a time.

Christine and I entered together.

Although the whole hospital smelled of carbolic soap and and floor-polish the smell was very much stronger here. On the wall facing the washroom door were four washbasins above which were four mirrors. Above these were two narrow windows high above eye-level. To the left of the washbasins were two roller-towels. The remainder of that room had a ledge running along one of the walls and above the ledge were hooks where each girl hung their comb, their toothbrush and their face flannel. Each of these had a tag with their owner's name on it. Toothpaste and a rinsing glass were set on the ledge beneath.

Christine showed me where my hook was.

To the right of us were four toilets. They were open and offered no privacy to the user.

"The nurses need to be able to see us all of the time," Christine said.

Then on the wall to right of the toilets was a very large shoe-rack, with a capacity for forty pairs of shoes. To the left of the toilets was a small window that looked out towards the cookhouse and this window was kept open at all times unless the weather was extremely bad. Placed on the floor beneath the window was a wooden box with '*Show Shine*' written on it in bold black letters on it.

Christine saw me looking at it.

"Girls like to volunteer to shine the shoes, because they want to hear news from nurses talking on the path outside."

She motioned towards the windows but where no voices came.

"There are three shoe-shiners," she said, "the first to put on the polish, the second to brush it off and the third to dust up a shine..

I washed my face and cleaned my teeth.

"You will need your comb now, carry it with you" Christine said, and so I took mine from its hook.

We next queued in order of height as I had seen the patients do before.

After the washroom we made our way to the dining-room and queued until we were allowed to go in. Then with everyone clutching their combs we entered.

The dining-room fire was always lit and putting out a good heat. Christine closely attended me because we were were exactly the same height, though she had brown hair and deep blue eyes with dark lashes. She was however thinner than I was and also I had darker brown hair and mine were brown eyes.

In our fours we walked beside our trestle table and seated ourselves on the benches. Ready on the trestle-tables were day-clothes that the girls had folded neatly the previous evening. Nurse Mollett had brought me my clothes and we

30

all soon dressed in the firelight, where we seemed glowing with warmth.

Then the door swung open and Sister Devereaux stepped gracefully into the room. Thoughts of how she had shaken me to the core came painfully back to my mind.

She was carrying a pile of opened mail that she placed on her desk. Once again I noticed how slim she was. She looked so fragile and I felt sure if someone had given her a big hug then she might have snapped in two.

She glanced around the room and on seeing Nurse Mollett Sister smiled radiantly, to my absolute surprise. Nurse Mollett was even smiling back at her. I marvelled that nurse Mollett could find it within herself to smile so warmly when Sister had been so rude the previous day.

Sister Devereaux then addressed us.

"Good morning," she said before sitting down. Then as Christine had just whispered to explain Sister began to read the night report made out by Sisier Kilshaw.

During her reading i was able to observe Sister more closely.

Sister Devereaux looked to be in her mid thirties. She still had the bloom of youth in her face, but I would not have considered her pretty because her face was so thin, Her cheekbones were too hard and her nose a little too sharp. She nevertheless had fine features that would have been more evident if her face had not been so lean. I noticed also that she was biting her bottom lip in concentration and I saw that her upper teeth were very slightly prominent.

Her outstanding features were her large expressive eyes. They were blue and accentuated by thick lashes and they indicated every facet of her every mood. I had assumed that she was incapable of smiling for she had seemed so cold and stiff. Yet that morning that icy stare was gone, replaced with a gentleness that gave her an air of attractiveness.

Eight chairs were next set out, four to each side of Sister's desk, for we all had to queue in order of height and sit on the chairs four at a time.

The first four chairs were for temperature checks and medication, and the second four chairs were for having our hair combed. Then after these procedures and at long last it was finally breakfast time.

We sat on our benches and listened to the rattle of the trolley coming down the corridor. The dining-room door opened and a lady from the cookhouse entered dragging a large trolley bearing tea urns and large pans of steaming hot porridge. The plates and mugs were the same grey aluminium ones that I had seen the previous day, though this time I did not mind because I was so hungry. My breakfast was placed in front of me and I picked up my spoon - eager to begin eating - but then slowly put it down when all of the girls closed their eyes and put their hands together and chanted in unison:

'For what we are about to receive, may the Lord make us truly thankful.'

Then everyone began to eat, and the porridge tasted good.

Whilst eating my breakfast I looked around me.

Many of the girls had haircuts almost as short as mine, and I did not feel so unpleasant any more. Then some of the other girls at my table began talking to me and asking where I was from, and I discovered to my complete astonishment that I was being treated as an equal. I was no longer the outcast, as I had been at school.

I smiled at Christine.

"How friendly everyone is," I said at last.

"It is important that we all try to get on as much as possible, Eleanor," Christine said. "Sister Devereaux has her rules and we must obey them.

This caused me to flinch and to glance away towards that desk.

"I don't want to talk to Sister Devereaux again," I said.

"Don't worry," Christine said. "Although Sister is a bit of stickler at times she is basically alright."

Then she looked towards the desk herself.

"She is strict but fair," Christine said.

I could not believe that Christine could defend such a rude and arrogant person.

"I will never ever like her," I growled.

Then came the voice of Sister Devereaux addressing everyone.

"Quiet please," Sister Devereaux said.

Then Sister turned and picked up a letter from the pile.

"Alice Lavery," she called out, and then a girl who was obviously Alice Lavery walked over to the desk and eagerly took her letter from Sister.

Sister continued to call out names, and then one of the letters was for Christine and then it was Christine who sat down with her letter and was sat bent over and quietly reading it.

My eyes burned with tears, because I too wanted a letter from home. I was homesick. I felt like I was floundering in an invisible ocean of despair.

Then all at once I became aware of someone standing in front of me, and when I looked up I saw a blonde haired, blue-eyed vision of loveliness was smiling down at me.

She took my hand in hers.

"I am Nurse Owens," she said in a sweet Welsh voice. "I would like to talk to you."

I was unsure what to do. I did not want to leave Christine, for she was my anchor and my friend. I looked to Christine but who remained lost in her reading.

Nurse Owens spoke again.

"Shall we go somewhere quiet where we won't be disturbed?" Nurse Owens asked.

I agreed, for that would at least be away from Sister Devereaux.

I allowed Sister Owens to usher me out of the dining-room, down the corridor and into Patience Ward.

Patience Ward had a small fireplace to my right with a cheery fire burning in the grate. Either side of the fireplace were two beds and then five beds opposite these that were neatly made. A French window overlooked the front grounds, while in the middle of the room was a desk and chair.

Nurse Owens seated herself in the chair and she pulled me onto her knee and hugged me closely. I buried my face in the bib of her apron and I cried. She dropped a kiss on my forehead, stroked my short hair.

"Now what are all these tears about?" she asked me.

I removed my face from her apron and looked up at her. I found myself relaxing as if her voice was a song.

Nurse Owens looked to be around nineteen years old and had the looks someone I had previously only seen on the silver screen of the cinema - though her face was devoid of make-up. Her hair was corn-coloured and though it was pinned up under her cap I could see it was long. Her eyes were china blue and fringed with long blonde lashes and she had a generous mouth with even white teeth, so that I felt myself instantly warming to her.

My story came tumbling out amid my tears and sobs, and I practically told her word for word my initial encounter with Sister Devereaux and how she had spoken cruelly to Nurse Mollett, and when I reached the end of my sad tale I looked at her expecting her to be shocked.

I was very surprised to find her smiling.

"You have absolutely nothing to worry about," she said before she gave her explanation.

"Seeing Nurse Mollett rebuked was unfortunate to see but let that be that," she said.

Then she paused.

"What I ask you consider is what Sister Devereaux saw directly in front of her." Nurse Owens said. "For she was faced with a silent little girl who had refused to speak or even look at her."

She stopped my complaint with her hand.

"Now Sister Devereaux has her own ways and she is rather blunt but only to find out who you really are," Nurse Owens said.

Nurse Owens gave me a little shake.

"Now have I said anything that is understood?"

I mumbled a reply.

"It still doesn't explain why she was so mean to me?"

Nurse Owens gave a sigh of exasperation.

"Sister Devereaux had been standing in front of a jellyfish and she wanted to know if you had a backbone, and only when you stared her square in the face did she find what she wanted: a little girl who could fight and overcome all that might try to weaken her."

Nurse Owens shifted her positions a little and held me closer.

"Sister Devereaux would practically lay down her life for any one of the girls here. I promise that when you get to know her a little you will change your opinion entirely."

I made such a sour face in reply.

"I will never - ever like Sister Devereaux," I saidSister Owens made a sour face of her own.

"Well Sister does have a quick temper - I grant you that - but she very soon forgets the cause of it. You are lucky to be placed in the hands of such an expert, whether you like her or not."

I breathed a sigh.

"But I am frightened of her."

Nurse Owens frowned.

"Let me tell you a story."

I sat ready and she began.

"My cousin, who is in the Royal Air Force took me to see a Halifax Bomber that was stored in a hangar. The hangar was large and that plane only just fitted in - wingtip to wingtip. Now the Lancaster Bomber was even bigger than the Halifax. Now consider instead the Spitfire, a tiny little plane, and yet it is a force to be reckoned with in the sky. Indeed there are some of the opinion that without the Spitfire we might not have won the war at all. Yet that little plane looks like a sparrow compared to the other two."

Then Nurse Owens came close to whisper.

35

"Sister Devereaux is your Spitfire, Eleanor. She will protect you no matter what."

I told Nurse Owens that I had understood a little.

Next she told me about the ward we were in, which was Patience Ward, which was mainly for five year olds and who were in the dining-room with the rest of them.

Then Nurse Owens and I left Patience Ward and we strolled along the corridor.

"You see it was Sister who asked me to have this little talk with you, because Sister noticed you were upset, and she would not notice these things if she was not nice."

Then when I was returned to my place in the dining room another strange thing happened.

Sister Devereaux's pile of letters had been distributed and everyone who had received one was quietly reading. That was when Sister Devereaux motioned to me to come and sit on a wooden chair that had been placed by her side.

"Come sit by me, Eleanor," she said as I approached, patting that wooden chair, so that I was soon seated right beside her.

"Just a few ground rules that I expect you to obey - and you needn't look so worried," she said.

She seemed a different person then, so friendly amd approachable.

"I want you to try your best to be a good person. I don't expect you all to be best friends, for every person has their likes and dislikes when it comes to personalities. Nevertheless, even if there is no common ground between two girls there is no reason why they should not treat each other with respect. You must not be selfish. You must learn to share with other girls any comics, books and toys that you are sent from home. Whilst I do allow for differences of opinions to be openly discussed, I will not tolerate girls falling out or fighting with each other. If they do, they are disciplined. You will be with them all of the time, therefore you are to regard them as a family unit, and in addition," and paused, "new patients are always welcomed warmly. I notice

36

you have already made friends with Christine Hastings. That pleases me. Now you may go."

With that she turned to the paperwork on her desk and paid me no further attention whatsoever.

I returned to my seat next to Christine with a feeling of relief.

"I told you Sister was ok," Christine said. "But you must be careful, because she is very strict, especially when a girl misbehaves."

I decided then that as I was quiet and shy and always striving to please, that there would be little chance of me finding myself in her disfavour. How wrong I was, as I was to discover on numerous occasions during my stay at the hospital.

Sister Deveraux rose and called for our attentions.

"As usual I request that no letters are left lying around, please put them away in your lockers. Fortitude girls - your walk today will be to the park."

Everyone filed out through the door, but before we passed through it we had to drop our soiled hankies into a box and pick up clean one from another box, whilst Nurse Mollett watched. One girl told the nurse she had lost her hankie, so Nurse Mollett told her to go to Sister Devereaux's desk.

Christine drew me aside.

"A girl will even steal another girl's hankie, Eleanor," whispered Christine, "rather than be stood in front of Sister's desk."

I held tightly onto Christine's hand as we went into Fortitude Ward where she put her precious letter from home in her locker. Then all us assembled in the washroom where we exchanged our slippers for a our day shoes. Next we collected our coats and our hats from the cloakroom, and then returned to the dining room for Sister Devereaux to inspect us to ensure we looked smart and have our coats brushed if necessary. She was completely intolerant of a lack of personal attention to neatness, and a badly fastened shoelace, or an unfastened button resulted in a sharp reprimand.

Next she inspected our shoes to ensure the shoe cleaners had done their job properly, and then a few minutes later we were walking through the cloakroom and out of the back door of the hospital for our walk.

It felt good to step out into the crisp cold air. The sky was blue and the low sun was making the frost on the ground glisten.

We walked in pairs in order of height, my partner being Christine, and with a nurse at the front and rear.

"How long have you been at the hospital?" I asked Chrsitine when we had walked some distance.

"Six months," she replied.

I looked at her in astonishment.

"Well my mam told me I would be home again in three months."

Christine met my gaze.

"Fortitude girls are rarely in for less than six months," she said. "They are sometimes in for even longer. Connie, my friend, you understand, was in Fortitude for a whole year."

I stared at her.

Then Christine added.

"It all depends on the doctors, you see. Connie, well she had two medicals and failed both," at this Christine looked away. "And each time she thought it would all be over with."

We walked in silence, she no doubt considering the subject as deeply as I did.

Then at last I decided to start a new conversation.

"What will we do after the walk?" I asked.

"It will be school next," she said. Then when looked at me she perhaps understood how lost I was.

"Shall I tell you the timetables for weekdays and Saturdays and Sundays?"

I nodded eagerly.

What she told me is listed here, but she recited it like she was remembering Tennyson.

Weekdays.

6.30 Wake up.
7.00 Rise, then Washroom and and toilet. Get dressed.
Temperature, medicine, hair combed.
8.30 Breakfast. Hankies.
9.00 Walk.
11.00 School.
12.00 Meal.
12.30 Rest on beds.
13.00 School.
14.00 Walk.
16.00 Showers.
17.15 Teatime.
18.00 Playtime.
19.00 Bedtime.
19.30 Light out - no talking.

Then Christine pretended to be exhausted.

"Saturdays are the same but with no school."

Then Christine's smile disappeared and she theatrically assumed a dour face and recited the Sunday timetable with a slow sanctimonious voice.

Sundays.

6.30 Wake up.
7.00 Rise - Washroom, Toilet, Get dressed . Temperature.
Hair combed.
8.30 Breakfast.
9.00 Walk
10.30 Chapel
12.00 Meal.
12,30 Rest for half an hour.
13.00 Walk
14.30 Church of England with Canon Robson.
16.00 Showers.
17.15 Teatime with two biscuits.
18.00 Gospel Hall preacher in the concert hall.
19.00 Bedtime.
19.30 Lights out.

Christine then cast me a look of dread.

"Sunday are really really awful," she reminded me.

We walked around the medium sized park that had grassed areas and flowerbeds containing a few struggling flowers. A gardener was busy raking up autumn leaves and I could see in the far corner a wispy coil of smoke rising whilst the fragrant smell of burning leaves hung in the air.

Not many regular people were in the park, just a few lone men and women walking their dogs.

After playing on the swings for a while we returned to the hospital, our crocodile causing the view visitors to stop and watch as we passed by.

Chapter 5.

The official schoolroom entrance could be found by leaving the building through the back door and then taking a pathway. However only the general public on open days entered the schoolroom by that way. Instead we used the short cut through a door in Courtesy Ward.

Courtesy Ward,when you passed by it, never had a finished appearance. The central-heating in Courtesy Ward looked as if it had been installed as an afterthought, for the thick pipes were not concealed under the floorboards but instead clearly visible running along the skirting-boards and up the wall right of the rear window and disappearing into the ceiling. There the pipes were lagged and in places the lagging was unfurling in a snake-like manner.

There were nine beds there, but only two of them were on that day occupied, both patients being fast asleep.

One of the windows of Courtesy Ward overlooked the front gardens and the other overlooked the rear grounds. There was a desk and a chair in the centre of the ward, as I expected.

The schoolroom was a small connected building that had its own proper entrance, as I have said, to the rear of the hospital. Three of the schoolroom walls had large paned windows stretching from about four feet from ground level to within six inches of the ceiling. This made the schoolroom very light and airy, whilst its heating pipes were orderly as they should be. The room was oblong but could be made into two rooms by a sliding partition that had solid wood panels on the lower half and glazed panels in the upper. That day it was folded concertina-style against the wall. The rest of that wall was dominated by a blackboard and then a bookcase that was full to capacity with children's books, and they were books that could be read at will. The remainder of that wall was taken up with children's paintings and drawings. There were no fixed desks, just stackable tables and chairs.

A wind-up gramophone stood on a table in one corner, The deck consisted of a turntable, covered in green baize, and then a rather lavishly styled pick-up. A fresh needle had to be installed each time a record was played. In the left hand front corner of the deck was a speed regulator by which one could adjust the speed of the revolutions of the turntable. There were a number of little trays on the deck that could hold new and spent needles. A small stack of records was also on the table.

In future lessons I was to discover that every single record was classical. For a ten year old girl like myself the music was initially intensely boring, since I had only ever heard the popular tunes of the day on our wireless. However, over the coming months I began to develop a liking for certain composers, my favourites being Tchaikovsky and Prokofiev. An appreciation of classical music remained with me ever since.

On my first day there our teacher introduced herself as Miss Moran and that morning we were to have English lessons. The hour was quickly gone, and then it was mealtime.

Christine and I walked together to the dining-hall.

"Miss Moran teaches five to ten year olds, and then there is a Mrs Barker who teaches eleven to fourteen year olds," Christine explained.

After mealtime we all had to lie on top of our beds quietly for thirty minutes, and each of us was cocooned in a single blanket. If the girls began to talk then Sister Devereaux would rat-a-tat-tat on the dining room window and impose silence.

Turning my head and seeing as there was nothing else to look at I came to take a good look at Fortitude Ward.

There was no form of heating there. The floor in this ward was bare concrete - no linoleum covering and mats as there were in other wards.

Arranged in three rows of six were eighteen beds. Straw mattresses (or pallets as they were sometimes called) were surprisingly comfortable and warm. They assumed the shapes of one's body, like a comfortable old shoe, and made a scrunching sound as we climbed in or wriggled to turn over.

The longest interior wall was about three feet high with windows fitted above that height, which gave a view of the corridor. Fortitude Ward was set lower than the other rooms, as I have said, for there were two steps that led up to the exit to the corridor that ran beside it. To the right of Fortitude Ward, as a passerby on the corridor might see us, was Patience Ward, while to the left, as I have already explained, was the dining-hall. Both the dining hall and Patience Ward windows allowed others to look down on where we lay..

The fourth wall. Which was exterior, was again about three feet high but had a huge sheet of wire netting fixed across it. Flat hinged shutters, which could be be raised up by ropes and pulleys until they were nearly flat to the ceiling. These were lowered at night time but they only blocked the top half of the netting, the bottom half giving the ward full exposure to the elements.

I was later to discover that when it was raining with a westerly wind then the rain would spatter fiercely inside the ward and staff would need to push the beds as far back from the netting as they could. In a heavy rainstorm I was to see the concrete floor awash with rainwater while our counterpanes were damp. Thunderstorms were especially frightening, and they were made all the more awesome by the fact that we were totally unprotected. We were all of us fearful lest a jagged fork of lightning should find us. Hailstones would clatter noisily about the floor and rattle the shutters while full downpours would cause rain to bounce about the exposed floor.

Surprisingly, during my stay in the hospital I cannot recall ever catching cold, and in warmer seasons I actually loved sleeping out in the open. On late summer nights when the shutters were not so low one could gaze at the moon and stars and wake to the new light and the birds' choruses. In summer too there was always the fragrant scents from the gardens and the fresh mountain breezes that arrived across the River Dee from Wales.

Following our rest period that day we went on our second walk of the day, after which we queued in the corridor for the bathroom in which there were two showers and a bathtub. Patients went in and out pretty quickly, for a duty nurse ensured we all spent a minimum amount of time bathing. On that first full day I was aware that the evening before I had been dreading meeting these girls.

One day had sharpened my awareness so much.

I was slowly beginning to remember some of the girl's names. Which allowed me to talk to them. One girl told me she had some comics that I could borrow during playtime and I thanked her. Other girls began speaking to me too, telling me their names and smiling.

I was also trying to appreciate the number of dialects I was hearing, since the girls came from all over the country. There was Sandra, who had a burr in her speech, whom I understood later was from Glasgow. There were dialects from Wales, Northumberland, the West Country, Birmingham while others I could not guess at all unless I was told.

I was the only girl with a Yorkshire dialect.

After my shower a dig in the ribs caused me to turn to find a sandy-haired girl with green eyes who asked me if I knew any exciting stories. She introduced herself as Flora Wilson, saying she was ten years old and from Northumberland.

Hers was called a 'Geordie' accent.

"I am Flora," she said confidently. "So do you know stories you can tell in bed during talking time?" she asked, her voice having such lovely deep tones. "Scary ones suit us best, mind!" she added.

I immediately felt at ease with Flora because of her high-spirited charm. I hoped that she too would become my friend.

"Just so you know," said Flora impishly, "to put you in the way of a really scary one," she said and she turned to stare into the distance. "There is the strangest door near the fire-exits, just up there," she added, "that no one has ever seen open."

Then she took my arm.

"I will show you," she said.

We walked away from the others until near where the corridor ended there was a plain door.

"It leads to somewhere, but not a cupboard and not place that has windows or steps as there is nothing here below us," she explained with a suitable tone of suspense.

Then she gave that door a long look.

"What do you suppose comes out of there when we are all tucked away in our beds?" she asked me.

Then she acted like it did not matter.

"Though they do say there is a ward in there where the children are made into monsters!"

It was a suggestion that quite thrilled and frightened me.

Then Christine approached and chided Flora for trying to frighten me.

Flora made light of it.

"I was only having a bit of fun," said Flora who looked dismissively at Christine, who by nature was charged to protect me.

Then Christine came to advise me as she so often did.

"As fun and mischievous as Flora is, Eleanor," she said, "she does well not to fall foul of Sister Devereaux more often than she does."

Then Christine paused for thought.

"But it is true what Flora says. There is no one knows where that door leads, because no one has seen it open."

"Then what do the nurses say?" I asked.

Christine stared at the door.

"The nurses say behind that door is nothing we should be concerned about."

Then we headed back to join the others while Christine satisfied my curiosity some more.

"The fortitude girls are apt to call it The Forbidden Door," she said, "and some of the older girls do tell stories about it at bedtime."

I looked back.

"Maybe it is just a cupboard," I said.

"If it was a cupboard the nurses would tell us that wouldn't they," said Christine.

We were soon back in line again.

"We simply do not think of it," Christine said and in time it was our turn for the showers.

Chapter 6.

Following our bathing we all lined up outside the dining room door waiting for permission to enter. Then on entering we walked along to our benches, the tallest ones finishing up on the bench under the window, the little ones by the door. Us 10 year olds were stood before benches that were exactly opposite Sister Devereaux' desk.

We sat down when she gave the order and then the now familiar trolley lady trundled in. The meal was sandwiches and a mug of tea. After our meal the trolley lady returned to clear up the dirty mugs and plates, so that now it was playtime.

Sister Devereaux called for quiet and then spoke.

"Enjoy your playtime, girls."

Then she cast her eyes over all of our faces.

"As usual I ask that you behave yourselves. Unfortunately for Connie Worrall there will be no playtime tonight, Approach my desk, Worrall."

Connie Worrall walked over to Sister Devereaux's desk and everyone quietly watched with great interest.

Connie stood with her back to us, so we could not see her face, but I could imagine what she was feeling.

Sister continued.

"As you are all too well aware, material is rationed. Lost handkerchiefs are hard to replace, and it is therefore imperative that you ensure you do not lose them."

She then spoke directly to Connie.

"I will not tolerate such negligence, Worrall. You are to retire to bed at 6 p.m., thus forfeiting your playtime. Have you anything to say for yourself.?"

"I will try not to lose it again, Sister," said Conie in shaky voice.

"I am not asking you to *try*, Worrall," said Sister. "I am demanding that you comply and in the event of a recurrence you will find yourself deprived of playtimes for a longer period. Understood?"

"Yes, Sister," Connie replied unsteadily.

"Is that all you have to say, Worrall?"

"I could hear Connie sniffling and I knew she was crying, but still Sister persisted.

"Are you repentant?"

"Yes, Sister," came the tearful, almost inaudible reply.

"Then why am I not hearing an apology from you?"

Connied bowed her and replied meekly.

"I am sorry, Sister."

"You will retire to bed this instant," finished Sister.

Then all eyes were on Connie as she walked dejectedly out of the room.

Then after she had gone Sister addressed us again.

"Let this be a warning to you all. Enjoy your play."

Sister then returned to yet more paperwork and was seemingly ignoring us.

Then everyone dispersed and began to laugh and chatter with each other. The chairs by the hearth quickly emptied as children collected their treasured dollies and teddy bears.

Christine however remained by my side like a sentinel.

"They tear up old sheets for handkerchiefs, but they do not have so many old sheets left," she said. "Please - please Eleanor," insisted, "do not leave your hankie lying around."

I then remembered something from my home and I blurted it out

"My mam has to cut sheets lengthways and sew the outer edges together so they will last longer in the rationing," I said, which seemed more complicated a description than it needed to be.

Christine raised her eyebrows.

"Well listen to you - the girl that hates what Sister says and does," she said mockingly.

I winced.

"Well I do not hate her," I said uncomfortably, "but I do not like her either. I am just saying that I understand why she got cross, because my mam gets cross too - about rationing."

Then I added some more.

"It was harsh of Sister to call her Worrell, and to send her to bed early," I said.

Christine had me follow her about.

"Sister is strict with every patient," she said.

Then out of nowhere she referred to her own home life.

"I am an only child, Eleanor, I have no brothers or sisters."

I responded immediately.

"I have a sister who is five," I said.

We spent time comparing dolls and then she appeared to remember something.

"I have made a doll of my own," she said. "I will go and fetch her."

Christine left the dining room to fetch the doll from her locker. She could not have been gone for more than a couple of minutes, but during that time I felt dreadfully alone. The rest of the girls were talking and playing and were quite oblivious to me standing alone. Even Flora was too busy with Anne to notice me there. I looked at Sister Devereaux and at that very moment she looked directly at me. I quickly averted my eyes, terrified that she might summon me to her desk.When I raised my eyes she was once again attending to her paperwork.

I felt such relief when Christine returned. She was carrying a small cardboard box and inside was a tiny doll.

"I made her from pieces of white scrap fabric," she said. "I cut them out and then I sewed them together. That yellow wool I glued on is her hair. She is called Daisy," she said proudly.

To say I liked the doll was an understatement and I wished she was mine.

"Can I pick her up?" I asked.

"If you are careful with her," Chrsitine said.

I very gently held the tiny doll and marvelled at the neat stitching. Christine had drawn a little face with blue eyes and ruby lips.

"She is beautiful," I said.

"Before I am discharged," Christine said, "before I go home, I will give Daisy to you," she said. "That is my solemn promise."

Then she saw what a change this had caused in me.

Then she returned Daisy to her box.

"Do you have any hobbies, Eleanor?" she asked me.

I felt uncomfortable answering her question, fearing that I would reveal the closed world I had at home.

"I like reading," I said.

"I like reading too," Christine said brightly. "But my favourite times at home are going to football matches with Daddy.

Her then seemed to soften in her recollection of happier days.

"He would hoist me up on his shoulders," and she showed me by lifting her arms, "so I could get a better view of the game. It was so exciting to watch and I would shout!" and she smiled. "Daddy posts me the sporting pages every week so I can check the results."

I was quite surprised that such a placid girl had sporting interests. I had loathed games lessons at school. It occurred to me then that if we had met outside of the confines of the hospital that we might have had hardly anything in common at all. However in here, in this place, we blended perfectly.

Christine was full of tact and diplomacy and responsibility and always seemed to have an insight into how I was feeling. I always felt extremely grateful to her.

Sister Devereaux announced it was time for bed and we reluctantly put away our toys and fetched our nightclothes from our lockers in Fortitude Ward and returned with them. We undressed, folding our day-clothes carefully in a neat pile on the tables, the nurses helping the five year olds.

Sister then bade us all goodnight and we went down the corridor to bed in Fortitude Ward. The nurses came round tucking us in, and although the air was cold we were all wrapped up tightly against the draughts.

There was then that half an hour talking time before sleep.

One of the older girls said she had the latest issue of "Sunny Stories," and asked if we would like her to read us one.

We all chanted: *"Yes please,"* in unison and I lay engrossed in a little story about Enid Blyton's Famous Five.

Christine and I loosened our arms from our bedding and we held hands as we listened. I had only known Christine since that morning, and yet I felt very close to her and hoped she would not go home before I did.

Then next the lights were switched off, but as Fortitude Ward was sandwiched between the dining-room and Patience Ward there was still plenty of light entering through the opposed windows and then from the dimmed lights beyond the corridor windows.

I could see the heads and shoulders of the day shift nurses gathered in the dining room. They all stood with their backs to Fortitude Ward so that only Sister Devereaux would be facing us. We could hear Sister reading a prayer. A hymn was sung, accompanied by someone playing the piano. Then they all walked out of the dining-room and those lights were switched off.

All of the day nurses across the hospital were going off duty and passing down the corridor. They had taken off their uniforms and were dressed in their own clothes. I saw Nurse Owens, walking down the corridor with her blond hair tumbling about her shoulders. I thought how beautiful she looked.

Then turning in our beds we saw nurses from the entire hospital walking on the street and mingling with a group of young men. The men had been standing by the gates and waiting for the pretty day nurses to come off duty.

Christine wriggled some way out from the bedclothes to look out through the mesh.

"The boys like the Welsh nurses the best," she whispered. "The nurses here are either from Liverpool or from across the river in Wales."

With the day shift over the night shift had begun. The night staff consisted of Sister Kilshaw, a middle aged woman with grey frizzy hair, and then one other nurse who was called the night nurse. Sister Kilshawwore the same uniform as Sister Devereaux. The night nurses wore a slightly different uniform to that of the day nurses. The night nurses had a large starched cap that was folded in two, corner to corner, in the manner of a headscarf. The two loose ends were tied back with a fastener while the third end joined the other two and hung down her back. On the front of her cap was a red cross. A larger red cross was also on the bib of her apron.

Just as she had done the evening before, Sister Kilshaw walked slowly around Fortitude Ward, carefully inspecting every girl, saying *God Bless* to the girls who were awake. Christine and I both reached out our hands to her and she grasped them.

"Good night - and - God bless," is what she said to us.

Sister Kilshaw spoke in a faltering, nervous fashion. She was often pausing as if she found it difficult to find the right words and she filled the gaps with many 'um's and erm's. Her shoes had rubber soles and she moved silent as a shadow around the ward.

Sister Kilshaw was a gentle soul.

Then with these confirmations of the night complete I found that long day had tired me and very soon I was asleep.

Chapter 7.

I awoke in the morning to the sound of enamel bowls being placed beside our beds and of nurses loosening our bedclothes. Leaning over the side of my bed as I was instructed to do I began to cough, and Christine's statement that every day had the same routine flashed into my mind.

Then as the shadows of sleep disappeared, I realised that today was Saturday and it would be different from yesterday - there would be no school for one thing. How I wished it was a visiting-Saturday, but I had been informed by Nurse Owens that the next visiting Saturday would be November 15th, which seemed too long a time to wait.

I continued with my coughing whilst I wondered whether there would be a letter for me this morning. This made me cough even more vigorously. When the nurse told me I could cease coughing then I gratefully slipped back into the warm bedclothes again.

Christine was still coughing. I saw her leaning over the bed and she had her back to me. Her nightdress had worked its way up and could see a part of her lower back. Every bone in her back was sticking out and clearly visible, for she seemed to have hardly any flesh on her at all. Did Christine have the same illness as me. If so I wondered if my spine was as thin and as knobbly as hers.

Christine finally slithered back into bed and then I voiced my question.

"What is it that the doctors say is wrong with you?" I asked her tentatively.

"I am suffering from a chest infection," she said glumly.

I thought about this.

"I asked my mam what was wrong with me," I said, "and my mam said I had malnutrition."

I sat up.

"I looked for 'malnutrition' in the dictionary and it said I was undernourished."

Christine had no comment on this. Instead she told me how difficult it was to know anything here.

"I once asked Sister," she said, "and I was told that my medical file was locked away."

Many of the girls who were in Fortitude Ward had not been told precisely what was wrong with them. Unlike girls in Courtesy Ward, who all knew exactly why they were there. There was a 'Doctor knows best' attitude with regard to patients records in the hospital. As well as this visiting times and dates were restrictive, lest the excitement curtailed a child's recovery.

Later while seated in the dining room I heard the quick steps off Staff Nurse Briggs and come bustling in through the door, her starched uniform rustling as she moved. Then I remembered that she deputised on Sister Devereaux's days off.

She swept over to the desk, placed the open letters down on the desk and then she turned to us.

"Quiet!" she shouted at the top of her voice.

When Sister requested silence everyone immediately obeyed. Staff Nurse however had to repeat her request three times before she achieved total silence.

"I hope you will bear in mind that I will be letting Sister Devereaux know of any bad behaviour while I am in charge," she said, "and woe betide any of you if I am not obeyed!" she said loudly.

I felt a tremendous sense of relief that it was not Sister Devereaux sitting at the desk. I did not mind Staff Nurse Briggs shouting and bellowing, because for me it was far preferable to Sister's quiet voice and her authoritative manner.

Christine nudged me.

"Staff Nurse won't carry out any of her 'woe betides,' because Sister will not allow any one else to woe betide us," she said. "Though she could write our names down in her book, which would be really bad,"

All during medication and hair grooming Staff Nurse Briggs was chatting with Nurse Owens and Nurse Stubbs in a friendly manner. I listened with interest as they discussed what films they had recently seen and the younger nurses talked about boyfriends. Nurse Owens had been on a date to the cinema with yet another new boyfriend. She described in detail how the date had turned sour when her father had kicked up a fuss because she had stayed out later than he had stipulated. Then there was a lengthy discussion about fathers who forgot to notice that their little girls grown up into women. Nurse Stubbs, it appeared, had a crush on Doctor Lang who was based at several hospitals. When Staff Nurse Briggs happened to mention that he was on site that day then Nurse Stubbs immediately went dreamy eyed, saying she would have a walkabout during her break to see if she could see him.

Nurse Owens asked if he ever noticed her and Nurse Stubbs replied.

'Not yet, but I am hopeful."

Staff Nurse Briggs and Nurse Owens glanced at each other and laughed, much to the chagrin of Nurse Stubbs.

It was only when Sister Devereaux was absent that the nurses talked so freely. We all used to enjoy sitting and listening to them gossip to Staff Nurse Briggs, so that we learned the very latest intrigue.

After breakfast Staff Nurse turned her attention to the morning mail.

Letters to children were always opened and read prior to being given to the recipient. I was later to learn that this was to safeguard against children reading any distressing news, such as the loss of a much loved pet, that would lead to a decline. Parents were aware of this, and any letter that was considered unsuitable was returned to the sender with a cautionary note. I was also to discover the same went for letters written by patients, lest a request for discharge without medical approval should ensue.

Staff Nurse Briggs began to call out the names of the girls who had mail, mine being one of them.

I fetched the letter and I quickly the pulled the letter out of the envelope and read it. It was written by my mam and contained all the sorts of news, about my sister, and about the neighbours, and Kitty our family cat.

Mam said that due to running the shop, she and Dad would have to take turns to visit me, since someone had to remain behind the counter. They could not afford to close the shop. Mam said she would be visiting me on November 15th and was counting the days to seeing me again. Everyone next door also sent their love and said they were all missing me. Her letter ended with 'Lots of love from Mam and Dad,' and there were lot of kisses.

Then there was a P.S. saying many of the customers were asking about me, and the cobbler, who rented a shop next door to us, also sent his love. I had liked going into his shop because it had a fragrant smell of leather and sometimes he had let me watch him repairing shoes. He was a very nice man and this caused me some homesickness as I sat remembering. I pressed the letter to my nose and sniffed to try to detect an aroma of home, but it simply smelled of writing-paper and nothing more.

Christine carefully folded her letter and replaced it in the envelope.

She glanced at me briefly and then glanced again.

"I can remember when I received my first letter," sher said. "I enjoyed reading about everyone back home, though it also made me feel sad," she added. "It was if I was missing home even worse than before somehow."

Christine had put into words precisely how I felt.

"That is exactly how it is," I said through my turmoil.

Then Christine folded her arms.

"The first letter caused the most upset, but I can tell you it will get easier from now on."

When it was time for our walk, Staff Nurse Briggs glanced out of the window, and seeing the blue sky and sunshine she decided that a walk along the front would be rather nice.

Half an hour later we were strolling along a concrete promenade and looking across the River Dee to Wales on its far bank. On the distant horizon there was a misty, indistinct purple shadow that were the mountains of North Wales. Our crocodile had broken up somewhat, and nurses Whitely and Stubbs who were escorting us were less strict due to there being no traffic hazards.

I looked around as we strolled.

There were one or two people walking nearby and I also noticed an elderly angler sat at a stone jetty clothed in waterproofs and holding a fishing-rod.

He interested me, so I walked a little nearer. On his hands were fingerless gloves. By his side was a net, plus various boxes, all with their lids removed. I ventured still closer to try to see what was in them, and I saw that one box was full of hooks and floats and other bits and pieces I could not identify. Another box contained what I thought was his bait. An empty sandwich tin containing some loose brown paper wrapping and some banana skins was next to his open rucksack. He was sat in such happy silence, his eyes gazing out over the water, his rugged face relaxed with an expression of contentment and well-being. I wondered what his thoughts were, for he did not appear to be watching rod and line. It occurred to me then that at least fifty years separated he and I. His life was almost over, while mine lay all before me. He continued to sit as still as a statue, seemingly oblivious to my presence and so I quietly retreated.

I noticed also there were banks of seaweed at the water's edge where gulls were flocking voraciously seeking food. I could hear their shrill cries all around me whilst they soared, swooped and dived into the water. The near sand on this particular part of the beach was very dry and windblown, interlaced with couch and marram grass. The sand had piled up so much that it nearly reached the height of the promenade wall.

I breathed deeply and the characteristic smell of the seaside invaded my lungs. When I licked my lips I could taste a trace of salt. When I next looked around there no more passing people and the lines of the promenade led seemingly forever.

Christine was looking forward too, her eyes scanning the distances.

The she spoke.

"In the height of the summer, Eleanor, this beach is filled with people, for you can hardly fit a sixpence between the deck-chairs," she said,

We stood for a few moments enjoying the winter sunshine.

"Are you still homesick after your letter?" she asked me.

"I am feeling better now," I said.

She looked very relieved.

"I am glad you are not another Dorothy Green," she said while indicating towards a figure ahead of us. "She gets terribly homesick, though of course everyone does."

Then Christine sighed.

""It takes Dorothy a whole week to get over visiting day."

I tried to see who Dorothy was.

Christine came closer.

"That's her over there, stood next to the nurse."

I saw a fair-haired girl with a melancholy expression on her face. I promised myself then that I would strive hard to rise above homesickness and never let it reach such perilous depths.

"Then of course there is Isobella," Christine said. "She is an orphan from Dr. Barnado's Cottage Homes. She has settled down in the hospital very well because there is no mother and father to miss. She has is what is called a 'House Mother' who comes every visiting day without fail and Isobelle is always hugged and kissed by her."

"It must awful to be twice as alone here," I said.

I was mulling over this sombre thought when Flora's shrill voice seemed to pierce the air like the gulls' cries had.

"Can we look into the rock-pools?" Flora asked with great shows of excitement.

Nurse Stubbs came over to ask her what she wanted then after a conversation we heard Nurse Stubbs say:

"No you can't because it is too cold," she said, "and you might get your shoes wet."

Flora groaned in exasperation and assumed a sulky expression. Then noticing that we were stood watching she smiled playfully and walked over to the promenade railings. Then after climbing onto them with dexterous ease she performed a somersault over the railings into the high deep sand below.

Nurse Stubbs hurried over to her, and after chiding her she walked away, leaving Flora with a sullen expression once again.

The angler seated on the jetty called across crabbedly.

"For goodness' sake keep the noise down! You will be frightening the fish!"

Flora's eyes turned in his direction and then to my absolute horror she stuck her tongue as far as the roots would allow an then stared spitefully at him.

The angler, preferring not to voice his thoughts, looked away. While Christine hurried over to Flora to talk with her.

I looked in the direction of the nurses, and by some amazing chance it seemed neither of them had witnessed the encounter. It would have been a event recorded and left on Sister Devereaux's desk. I shuddered at the thought.

Then feeling I should not be involved in further trouble I noticed Dorothy Green was now stood by herself and leaning on the railings and gazing thoughtfully out across the river, so I walked over to her.

Dorothy slowly looked at me with sadness in her grey eyes. She smiled wanly and then she returned her gaze to the water.

"When I am discharged," she said plainly, "I never want to see The Wirral ever again."

I remained silent, waiting for her to continue/

"I hate the place," she finally said. "I hate the hospital. You would rather be at home, wouldn't you?"

I thought for a moment.

"Have you made any friends?" I asked her.

"My truest friends are back home," she said, while she ran her fingers through her blonde hair in an agitated fashion. They are back home and not in this prison."

Then she made a stricken face.

"Sister Devereaux threatened me with fewer visiting days if I refused to be friendly."

She spoke of Sister Devereaux as I thought of her. It was somehow reassuring that we felt the same.

Dorothy was very close to tears and I found myself at a loss as to how to reply,

I was saved, as it were, by Flora who bounded up to me, once again in a happy mood and telling me it was the ward concert that evening, and it was Fortutude's turn to put on a show.

"Could you sing a song?" she asked in her merry way. "Or would you know a poem you could recite to everyone?"

I was appalled at her suggestion.

"No Flora," I said in abject terror, " I could not possibly go onto a stage."

I looked to Dorothy for support but she had wandered off.

Then Flora, who obviously had no problem performing, seemed to find my position unimaginable.

"You don't have to do anything if you don't want to. But you would be better be off on stage with us than sat in the audience with girls you do not know?

This argument was extraordinarily compelling.

Then she angled her head and her green eyes were flashing.

"You are going to yes, I can tell," she said.

I found myself unable to refuse.

Flora gave a little twirl of triumph.

"Well, to begin with there are two porters' trunks backstage filled with costumes that have been given to the hospital. All we really have to do is dress up!" she said with glee.

Then she looked away with a slight smile.

"I will bet anything that Christine will sing *Swanee River*."

"Why are you so sure?" I asked.

"It is her favourite song," said Flora. "She gets called 'Swanee' because of it."

Then Flora seemed a little defeated.

"But she does sing it really well."

The nurses began shepherding us all together, since it was time to return to the hospital.

I had enjoyed my morning walk along the promenade.

A delicious aroma of cooking met me as I walked through the back door of the hospital, making me drool with anticipation of meal time. Indeed I sat down to my midday meal with enthusiasm.

Although my mother was a good cook, despite the restrictions of rationing, I could not recall ever having enjoyed a meal so much in my life before.

Perhaps simple fresh air day and night was having a beneficial effect after all.

Chapter 8.

At 5.45pm that evening we assembled in order of height in the corridor outside Fortitude Ward. Then permission was given to pass through the fire doors and down the long corridor. We went through numerous fire doors,and passing many side doors. Some of the side doors bore nameplates but I was none the wiser since the words were technical. On we walked as the rest of the girls were chattering happily, concentrating on each other rather than looking around, since they had obviously walked this way many times.

I had wondered where there might be stairs to the upper floor. Perhaps there were enclosed spaces hiding these stairs. Perhaps some of the side doors did lead to the stairs.

As we walked further it began to get warmer, then when we walked though a further fire door the heat met me, flowing over my body while there was a stronger smell of antiseptic in the air.

A whooshing sound to my right made me jump, and some doors slid open revealing an elevator out of which a stepped a nurse pushing a young girl in a wheel chair. The nurse then pushed the nurse in the opposite direction down the corridor.

We went through another fire door and a fresher atmosphere surrounded us. Further along I saw that one of the left hand side doors was slightly ajar, being held open by a nurse who was having a conversation with someone in the room. I could hear staff talking and laughing within. A radio was switched on and the happy refrain of 'Teddy Bear's Picnic' could be heard. A faint smell of cigarette smoke was drifting our way also, since the perils of smoking were not gone into so much in those days.

At long last, and after I had seen so many new places, we reached the end of the corridor where there was a door facing us with a nameplate that read: 'Concert Room.'

Upon entering the concert hall I was awestruck.

The stage was at the far end of the room and had deep red curtains. To the left of the stage stood a piano, where the floor was highly polished wooden parquet tile. A large number of stackable chairs were set out in rows to accommodate the audience, the remainder being stacked around the remainder of the room. Then I saw the ceiling was decorated with angels playing harps, and cherubs rising above clouds. Around the upper parts of the three walls was a frieze depicting the story of Cinderella, painted in fine detail. Below the frieze there were nursery rhymes illustrated, though they seemed dated in their style and content, even by the standards of those times.

We walked across the hall, then up four side steps onto the stage and into the wings. There, just as Flora had described, were two black trunks. One was marked 'BOYS,' and the other 'GIRLS.' We opened the latter and began pulling out the clothes and strewing them across the floor. There was practically every costume imaginable, from Cinderella's ball-gown to Little Bo Peep.

Amidst all the excitement the lady pianist had arrived and was going around with a clipboard trying to find out who required accompaniment and what tune. As my rendition was a poem, which required no accompaniment, I concentrated on the costumes, first trying on a fairy costume with wings. However when I looked at myself in mirror I looked more like a stick insect than a fairy, and so I tried on something else. I became a genie, a witch, then I saw a costume for a character from Longfellow, which I settled upon. It had a beige skirt and matching jacket, each with red fringes around the hemlines, and a red band to place around my forehead, which had a feather in it.

Dressing up in theatrical costumes was something I had never done in my life before, and the experience was marvellously exhilarating. I spent some time standing in front of the mirror, occasionally being pushed out of the way by the other girls. Eventually I had the mirror to myself and I was stood whispering my poem, trying to calm my nerves and deciding whether or not I should smile. I decided I should try to smile.

We were all ready. Behind the drawn curtain we could hear the audience taking their seats amidst the sound of chairs scraping on the floor and a babble of conversation. At 6.00 p.m. sharp the pianist stepped through the curtains and gave us a verbal introduction, after which she walked down the steps to her piano.

The curtains were opened, and the show began. Girls sang, recited poetry and danced. One girl even gave a gymnastic display with a few cartwheels.

I was stood in the wings awaiting my turn, and observing the audience. Practically every seat was taken, with nurses, Sisters, and a couple of doctors sitting at the back. Next to the nurses were boys and girls in wheelchairs. Then children took up the rest of the seating with the little ones at the front.

Christine was on now, dressed up as a gypsy girl, and as Flora had predicted, sang '*Swanee River*' in a sweet soprano voice and perfectly in tune.

Flora then took the stage, dressed as a pantomime chicken, and her turn was a routine involving singing rhyming words and gesturing to the parts of the body to which they referred. The chorus following each verse got longer and longer as happens with the famous song: '*This Is The House That Jack Built.*' After the second chorus everyone began to join in with Flora because they knew the words and they also mimicked her gestures. The whole concert hall rang with the sound of children singing at the tops of their voices. Then after her extraordinary performance Flora made a bow to thunderous applause.

It was me next, and what an act to have to follow!

I froze until someone behind me gave me a firm push, forcing me to take those few steps onto the stage where I was in full view of the audience.

The pianist announced my name, explaining I was a new patient.

I began my little poem entitled '*Butterfly,*'

I started nervously, but quickly gained control and upon finding myself relishing the theatrical camaraderie I recited the poem faultlessly.

At the end of the poem I gave a little curtsey.

Everyone applauded and I exited the stage.

A feeling of exhilaration ran through my body, such as I had never felt before. For the first time since my arrival I felt happy and among sincere friends.

Every Fortitude girl was patting others on the back saying 'Well Done! Well Done!'

High-spirited Flora had stolen the show, and I was so pleased for her, and I was proud to receive her praise for me and to call her my friend.

Chapter 9.

The following day was Sunday, and by the time the day was out I knew exactly what Christine had meant when she said it was monotonous. I was eventually to discover that Matron was firmly of the belief that the Sabbath should be kept Holy. Although she rarely went on walkabouts during the week, it was not uncommon to see her walking the corridors on a Sunday, checking that we were adhering to her rules.

At no time during the day were we allowed to speak or laugh loudly, and singing other than hymns was strictly barred. There was no play hour following teatime, instead we had to listen to a preacher from the local Gospel Hall give us religious instruction, after which he would give us a verse from the Bible to learn and recite the following Sunday. The whole day was steeped in religion, with children attending either the Catholic or protestant churches morning and afternoon.

At least we Fortitude girls had our twice-daily walks, which were a welcome respite from the sanctimonious atmosphere in the hospital. The only highlight of Sundays was that in addition to our sandwiches at teatime we were given two wholemeal biscuits.

Whilst my faith in God has never wavered, Matron's enforced religious instruction missed its mark and deterred me, and I imagine many others, from attending a church for many years after our discharge from hospital.

Chapter 10.

Our weekdays days were spent adhering to the daily timetable, only differing in where we walked and what lessons we had in the schoolroom. We even knew what we would be served for dinner each day, for there was a weekly menu. My days however were not spent unpleasantly, for Christine and Flora and I had become firm friends, enjoying each others' company immensely. Anne was also a member of our group, though she tended to play more with Flora than with me. This meant that I did not get to know Anne quite as well, but nevertheless I liked her.

Flora was such a happy girl, she seemed always to see the bright side of everything, and there was hardly ever a dull moment when she was near. Just occasionally however she would take offence at either a remark or an action where no offence was intended, and then she would sulk for a while. Being the cheerful girl that she was, she could not keep up her sulky mood for very long, and harmony was always very soon restored. Despite the fact that, like every other patient, she was unwell, she seemed able to generate more energy than the rest of us, for she was hardly ever still. She could not have a conversation without shuffling her feet as she talked, and she tended to gesticulate with her hands and arms. She had such wonderful green eyes that sparkled as she talked and were a part of her utterly charming personality.

Christine was quieter, more of a thinker than a doer and like me she never wasted energy if she could help it, for neither of us had reserves of energy to spare. Christine was very sociable and friendly and well liked by her peers, but at times she needed to have time to herself and would shun conversation in favour of settling down contentedly with a book. The time she reserved solely for herself never bothered me, for I too enjoyed reading. She always had empathy with the feelings of others, especially when they were suffering pangs of homesickness. When Dorothy, whom I had met briefly at the side of the river, had one of her black moods then it was usually Christine who was the comforter, or at least tried to be, for Dorothy was not improving.

Today however, Dorothy was in high spirits. She eagerly greeted the morn, ate a hearty breakfast, and for the first time I saw a genuine smile on her face. The reason was simple. Today was Saturday the 15th of November, the day when we were allowed visitors.

I too was exceptionally cheerful, for the prospect of seeing my mam again filled me with delight, and I simply could not wait to hug her and kiss her. My mother was travelling on service buses because she could not afford the train fare, but in her letters she assured me that she would be there at visiting time on the dot and was desperate to see me again and hear all of my news.

Visiting time came around. Those of us who were expecting visitors were seated in the dining-room, and girls who were not expecting visitors were taken for a walk. I felt sorry for those girls whose parents lived too far away to visit and I used to watch them as they walked dejectedly out of the dining-room. I felt so grateful that I was not one of them, though I was aware also how much they must have envied us. In the 1940's very few people owned a car, almost everyone relied on public transport, apart from those with middle and higher incomes.

At last 2.00 p.m. came around, and my mam walked through the dining room door with her arms held wide. I ran to her and she hugged me so tightly that I could hardly breathe. When we unclasped and looked at each other we discovered we were both in tears. How wonderful those 60 minutes were. I had so much to tell her, and she was very surprised to hear that I had made not one but two friends in the short time I had been in the home. She and Daddy had been so worried about me being a loner.

I looked at my mam. She had her fur coat on. The one Dad had bought her when they were courting. She also wore her new hat, the type that rests on top of the head and slightly over the forehead. When I said I liked it she confided:

"Your auntie loaned the hat to me on this special day, so that would be proud of me," she said.

"Mam," I said. "I will always be proud of you, hat or no hat!"

All too soon the hour was up, and it was a very tearful goodbye we had as she left the dining-room and turned down the corridor. I went to the dining room window and though it was an oblique angle to the road I waited for her to appear on the street and I waved and waved until she was completely out of sight.

A feeling of sadness now swept over me, and I desperately wanted to go home. Christine was exactly the same, as was Anne and Flora. It was the first time I had seen Flora in tears.

We were all subdued for the rest of the day, and not even the thought of the Saturday night concert could dispel my gloom. I was pleased when bedtime came around and I could release my tears in private.

In the days that followed I quickly overcame my nostalgia for home, as did everyone else, the exception being Dorothy. She was forever bursting into tears, and words of comfort made not one iota of difference. She did not even try to settle down like the rest of us, setting herself apart from us and looking pale and wan, and frequently shunning any attempts we made to involve her in our play.

I was also getting to know the nurses better and I loved it when they hugged and kissed us; I had never done so much hugging and kissing in my life before. Nurse Owens was my absolute favourite, for she was so pretty and caring. Every single girl liked, or even loved, Nurse Owens, and we all wished we looked like her. She loved us back and hardly ever got cross with us. She was also good with words, and tended to know just what to say when a girl was upset.

My second favourite was Nurse Mollett. She was not pretty like Nurse Owens. She had lots of acne spots on her face which caused me sometimes to pity her. However she was kind and gentle with endless patience and always managed to keep a smile on her face, even at times of stress. Her gentle charm endeared her to every patient. She wore those glasses with the thick lenses, the kind that people unkindly referred to as 'bottle tops,' They made her eyes look small. I noticed however that when she took her glasses off she had pretty hazel eyes.

Two other nurses interested me, mainly because of their personalities.

Firstly there was Nurse Whitely. She was tall, at around five feet seven inches, had auburn hair that waved naturally and had deep grey eyes. She tended to be over-sensitive and could not handle criticism very well, resulting in her shedding tears when she thought no one could see her. This was especially so when she had been on the receiving end of choice words from Sister. We used to hear her telling others nurses how she hated working at the hospital and was looking for employment elsewhere.

Secondly there was Nurse Stubbs. The reason why I took notice of her was because she was the one who opened her mouth and seemed to land herself right in it. She then looked to her friends and colleagues for help and support when she found herself in those embarrassing situations. She was always talking about Dr Laing, whom she adored, but who never looked her way, but it did not stop her from trying to attract his attention. She provided a lot of amusement for the other nurses, in fact I once heard Staff Nurse Briggs comment that their working days would not be half as interesting if that 'scatterbrain' was not around making everyone laugh.

Last but not least, there was Staff Nurse Briggs, who was younger than her features portrayed.

Many of the girls preferred her to Sister because although Staff Nurse Briggs shouted a lot, even bellowed at times, our days were more relaxed when she was deputising for Sister. Flora had told me once that the shoe cleaning girls had overheard that Staff Nurse Briggs' fiance had been killed in the war. Then although she dated regularly she never got emotionally involved because she still loved her late lamented. I felt sorry for her when I heard this sad little tale and began to like her too. She always walked about with a quick heavy step with her starch uniform rustling, and everyone knew when she was in the vicinity long before she came into view because we could hear her shoes approaching.

Then last but not least there was Sister Kilshaw, the sentinel whose kindly nature sent us to sleep with God's blessings. She had such difficulty with her speech, which marred by hesitancy and a stammer, yet of all those that spoke to me her words were the simplest and well meant.

The rest of the nurses performed their roles efficiently and thoughtfully but I never developed a closeness with any of them. I had become joined by the heart to them through their small kindnesses and the assuring fact that they would strive always to be there.

Chapter 11.

Nothing of consequence happened, until on the 20th of November, when, after breakfast, a small table was brought into the dining room and placed near the piano. Next the maintenance man came in carrying a wireless set that he placed on the table and then took the power cable along to the power socket. What was going on?

Sister informed addressed us.

"Today is the wedding of Her Royal Highness. Princess Elizabeth, heir to the throne, and Prince Phillip of Greece," she said. "Our timetables will be a little different in order that we can listen to the commentary on the wireless."

All the nurses were very interested, especially Nurse Owens. She came into the dining room carrying a glossy magazine and settling herself on the piano stool and began to thumb through it. Staff Nurse Briggs entered and walked over to see what Nurse Owens was looking at.

"Dream on girl," said Staff Nurse Briggs loudly, "you'll never have a Sir William Hartnell's wedding dress on your back."

"Unfortunately," replied Nurse Owens, "I cannot buy clothes of any description at the moment because I have used up all of my clothing coupons."

They both laughed.

A short time later we were all seated, listening to the pomp and pageantry of the occasion.

The commentator said:

"The gloom of post-war Britain has been lightened by a fairytale Royal romance."

Nurses were constantly entering the dining room to try to listen for a few minutes in between carrying out their duties, and for the remainder of that day that was all anyone talked about, with nurses saying they could not wait to see the Pathe News at the cinema.

It amazes me to think of the power of the radio in those days and that an occasion such as that could be conveyed simply with words. Our imaginations were being constantly fed and while daily routines might continue so long as the radio was within earshot. Whereas as newspapers had provided for a previous age it was the voice and storytelling that dominated ours, to the extent that even in our relative confinement we could travel to London and even further and be borne aloft by words in a way that was as common before or since.

Chapter 12.

I went into the washroom one morning as usual and completed the daily ritual of toilet, washing myself and cleaning my teeth, and as always I reached to take my comb from its hook but I was puzzled when I saw that the hook was bare. I looked away, and I returned my eyes to the hook, hoping that by some miracle the comb would be hanging there, but it wasn't. I stared unbelievingly, for where else could I have put it?

I slowly and thoughtfully replaced my toothbrush on its own hook, all the time my mind racing. I tried to mentally retrace my actions of the previous day, hoping I would remember where I was when I last held it in my hands, but I could not. What had I done with it?

Both Christine and Flora, who by now knew about my dilemma, helped me to search for it. We looked in every nook and cranny of the washroom, peering behind the radiator, underneath the washbasins, and even behind the toilets, but to no avail.

I went into Fortitude Ward and emptied out the entire contents of my locker, but my comb was not there either. Panic was now rising within me, and I returned to Christine and Flora who by this time were queueing outside the dining room and waiting for permission to enter.

I spoke with halting breath to the two of them.

""Someone could have stolen it," I said.

Flora whispered back.

"That would be very unlikely because the comb does have your name on it."

I knew what Flora had said was true, for the comb had a small hole at one end through which a small chain was threaded, which in turn bore an aluminium tag with my name etched onto it.

Christine turned around as much as she dared.

"Your only option is to simply admit that you have lost it, Eleanor, even though you will have to face the consequences," she said.

I was incapable of replying because I was frozen with fear.

Over the past few weeks not once had I done anything that had brought a frown to Sister's face, and I had thought that it would be no hard task to continue that way. I had even had the audacity to feel quite smug as I saw other girls standing before Sister being disciplined. Now, for the first time I realised that no one was perfect, not even me.

I began to wish that I was thousands of miles away, anywhere except standing without a comb outside the dining room. I was fearful of what Sister would say to me, but terrified also of what form the punishment would take. All of the other girls who had been disciplined had either lost their hankie or been naughty and were sent to bed early, but what would the penance be for a lost comb?

I shivered as a nightmarish thought entered my mind. Could this possibly be what the forbidden door was for? Maybe it was a punishment room for girls who committed a misdemeanour. I quaked with fear as I began to speculate whether girls were smacked in there, rather as my mother had spanked me when I was naughty. Maybe the punishment in that room was even worse, such as a cane.

The opening of the dining room door interrupted my thoughts and the girls began entering.

I stepped up onto the bench and walked with my shoulders sagging as we formed a queue for temperature, medication and hair combing.

My stomach was churning. I noticed Dorothy was crying again, and I felt a stab of impatience.What had she to cry about? I was the one with the big problem.

Sister Devereaux walked over to Dorothy and was talking earnestly to her whilst holding her hand. I thought that Sister would not be so understanding when my moment came.

Nurse Mollett who was on hair duty was surprised to learn that I had lost my comb.

I addressed her with a whisper.

"Could you give me another one without Sister finding out?" I asked.

"I am sorry, Eleanor, I cannot do that" said Nurse Mollett, "you will have to go and tell Sister what has happened."

With a heavy heart I approached Sister Devereaux's desk. She was at that moment talking to Nurse Owens, answering a query about medication, and Sister was smiling as she chatted.

She then turned to me.

"Yes, Eleanor?" she asked, still smiling.

I mumbled to her that I had lost my comb, watching for her smile to disappear.

Instead she said in soft tones: "Speak up Eleanor, I cannot hear you!"

I looked at her as steadily as I could and repeated more clearly.

"Please Sister, I have lost my comb!"

She was silent for a moment, solemnly looking at me and then she said sternly:

"Well! You had better go and find it hadn't you!"

I cringed.

"I have searched everywhere Sister," I said, "I don't know where else to look."

"Go and look again!" she commanded.

That was all she said; it was a simple statement, but her eyes spoke volumes.

So I looked yet again in all the places where I had already searched. I knew that I was not going to find it, and the only explanation I could think of was that I must have left the comb in my skirt pocket and then lost it while we were out walking. I returned to Sister's desk, heavy of heart and terrified of what her reaction would be.

"I still cannot find my comb, Sister," I said when I returned and was trying to control my trembling voice.

To my surprise, she made no comment, and instead she simply opened a drawer on her desk, took out a comb and said:

"Take this to Nurse Mollett for your hair grooming, then return it to me."

After Nurse Mollett had combed my hair I returned to Sister's desk with the comb, which she silently took from my hand and replaced in the drawer. Then, completely ignoring me, she turned to Nurse Owens and began speaking to her.

I did not know what to do, for she had not dismissed me, so I remained standing in front of Sister's desk.

Then she glanced at me and said coldly:

"Go and sit down, Eadie."

So I walked away, returning to Christine and Flora.

Christine and Flora were both full of questions.

"What did Sister say to you?" Flora asked.

I told them both what had taken place.

After this Christine thought for a moment, then leant in to me.

"Did she give you a replacement comb?" she asked.

"No, she didn't," I said.

Then with a solemn voice she pronounced upon the matter.

"Then you are still very much in trouble," she said.

I knew she was right.

To my surprise the rest of the day's schedule progressed as usual. During coat and shoes inspection Sister paid me no more attention than any other girl. It was the same at noon mealtime. Not once did Sister give any indication that I was out of favour. Teatime came, and after the dinner lady had cleared the tables I heard the clear and precise voice of Sister Devereaux saying:

"Eadie! Please approach my desk."

I had feared this would happen, yet when the command when it came felt like someone had punched me in the stomach.

I felt glued to my seat until Christine gave me a little push and I got up and walked over to Sister's desk, shaking with fear.

"Have you found your comb?" she asked, her face stern.

"No Sister I have not," I replied unsteadily.

"Whose comb is it?" she asked, keeping her blue eyes fixed on me, whilst I knew that the whole roomful of girls were at that moment watching the performance.

I was a little perplexed at the question, because she already knew that it was my comb that was missing.

After hesitating for a moment I replied:

"It is my comb, Sister.

"Wrong!" she said. "Any article issued to you by the hospital remains the property of the hospital, and we expect you to take care of such items. Combs cost money. Obviously you regarded this comb as a minor item that could easily be replaced, a misconception that you need to be made aware of. You have been grossly negligent, Eadie, haven't you?"

She fixed her eyes on me, waiting for my reply, but fear, plus the sternness of her face had numbed my brain.

She leaned forward in her chair and repeated.

"Haven't you?"

"Yes, Sister," I said in a timid little voice.

"Yes Sister what? She demanded.

"Yes Sister, I have been negligent," and then I added more, "I am sorry, Sister."

My final words seemed to appease her, for she chided me no further, and handed me a new comb with my name on it, then saying:

"Lose this at your peril."

Waiting with embarrassment I was observed by everyone as I given two early nights as my punishment

I left the dining room to get my nightdress out of my locker and to get changed for bed, yet at the same time I felt relieved that I had not been sent to The Forbidden Door.

For two nights I was in bed by 6 p.m., and I lay alone in Fortitude Ward hearing the other girls enjoying their play, while I bemoaned my lot.

After completing my early nights in bed, I began to study Sister a little more closely, and noticed that she never referred to the comb incident again; it was over and done with.

Although she was quick tempered. She often forgot the cause of her anger and she never bore malice - regardless of the misdemeanour. I could see now what Christine had meant when she had said that Sister was *'firm but fair.'*

This did not however alter my own view . a few weeks later I vehemently declared to Nurse Owens:

"I absolutely loathe Sister Devereuax and I will never ever like her!"

To this Nurse Owens replied:

"When you get to know her better I think you will change your opinion."

Some part of me trusted Nurse Owens above all others, so that I had to accept her view, as bizarre as it was, in case she might be right.

If Sister Devereaux was nice then I was completely at a loss to know where that niceness was going to come from.

Chapter 13.

Flora had first made me aware of the 'Forbidden Door' when we were in the corridor queueing for the shower room. I had been intrigued by what I had heard, both from the fanciful mind of Flora, and the common sense version told to me by Christine.

During the daytime I could never pass that door without pausing to stare at it. I had become fixed in my desire to know what lay behind it and why we had never seen it open. We had all tried the handle, but it was securely locked. I found myself giving some of the bedtime stories credence, completely discounting the possibility that it could be just an unused room, or even a cupboard. After all, if it was only a cupboard then why all the secrecy by the nurses?

The Forbidden Door was a favourite storytelling subject, and I would lie in bed tingling with excitement as tales of wild fantasies or the macabre would be narrated. The patients in Fortitude Ward were between six and fourteen years of age. It was always a child aged thirteen or fourteen who was selected as a storyteller for they could think up tales of a higher standard than the younger ones.

There was a maximum of twenty five minutes for the story to be told and so the story always progressed at a galloping pace and in a simple and matter-of fact fashion, but even so girls would reach out their hands to grasp the hands of others for reassurance.

Bedtime stories varied. It depended on what had been occupying our minds on a particular day, and also the weather and the season of the year played its part. A rainy day with a wuthering wind was far more inspiring than sunshine and warm breezes. There were also the many sights and sounds beyond our rather caged room too, for after the setting of the sun, when diurnal creatures took their rest, was when the nocturnal feeders replaced them. The street outside the hospital was tree lined, and on moonlit nights we used to watch the celestial orb travel across the sky behind the branches, while bats flitted there too.

During my time in the hospital the effectiveness of a story depended on the season of the year or else how much activity there was outside. Taking the seasons in general there were always those bats, lots of them. If one stared at a source of light, such as a gas lamp, the bats could be seen swirling , darting and swooping in their efforts to catch insects that were drawn to it. Then there were the hoots, screeches and kwick-kwicks of owls. Then of course those moths and other insects would fly into the ward through the wire netting, attracted by the corridor lights and then frantically skitter across the panes of glass. The buzzing and chirping of crickets was also a familiar sound. Occasionally the howling of a distant dog would add to the mental stimulation as a story was told.

Sounds with the hospital heightened the tension even further, such as the nearly silent footfall of a passing staff member in the corridor. The distant closing of doors could also sometimes be heard. Such sounds that no one takes the slightest notice of during daylight hours, caused one's mind to take flight when stories had us believe these sounds ominous.

During the late late spring and summer months when we went to bed in broad daylight the necessary backdrop for suspense was absent. Often holiday-makers would stand in front of the hospital looking at the grandeur of the building and then pointing in surprise at Fortitude Ward, for in their minds we were children were sleeping out in the open. So during the brighter evenings the tales were generally of adventure and mystery.

In the late autumn and and winter however we went to bed in darkness. The electric lighting in Fortitude Ward was very dim, so during talking-time those lights gave a atmosphere for danger and dread. These were tales of witches and giants, of ghosts and ghouls, or tales of the undead. There were stories of demon-doctors and wicked nurses that were very popular. Whatever form the story took, in winter or in summer, the Forbidden Door would frequently be featured. On a cold wintry evening the storyteller's breath would vaporise above them, a queer mist that surrounded her head and heightened the magical mood, whilst our own breaths made fountains in the dark frosty air.

A story could be about anything the storyteller wished, only there was one important rule: One of the girls in Fortitude Ward should feature in it. This increased the excitement even more as every girl waited, wondering if they should be named, especially if the tale was spooky.

At the end the storyteller always rewarded with rapturous applause.

I saw so many patients come and go in Fortitude Wars and yet the structure and intensity of the stories never varied, for new patients quickly learned the rules of those Fortitude bedtime tales.'

Unfortunately I cannot remember any of them, but I can vividly remember the thrill and the excitement that reigned during those twenty minute escapes into the inventions of children, now lost in the mist of time.

Chapter 14.

Letters from my mam were frequent, sometimes they were just hastily scribbled one-page notes, but for me they were priceless. They were the only link with the outside world - the world I had left behind. Sometimes I would think of home and wonder if it really existed, such was my life of sameness and regularity within the walls of the hospital.

In her last letter my man had told me that she would again be visiting me, because my dad was not well enough to make the journey at the moment. He was however, she assured me, making excellent progress, and he had been issued with a surgical shoe. His crutches were now gathering dust in the cupboard. I was so happy when I read this news.

I was glad my next visitor would be my mam, because I especially wanted her to hear us sing '*Silent Night*' the Christmas carol that the girls who were expecting visitors were busy rehearsing. I fizzed with excitement at the thought of how proud she would be of me. We were practising at every available moment, with Miss Moran and Mrs Barker giving the tuition. The girls who would were to sing the high notes were also singing the descant, while the rest of us were singing the traditional tune, and practice session by practice session it was beginning to sound rather nice. The plan was to assemble around the pianist and sing our hopefully perfect rendition for our parents as a surprise.

I felt sorry for the girls who would not be having visitors, and although Sister had forbidden us to talk about our singing treat in front of them, they nevertheless knew all about it. Secrets were difficult to keep when we were together every hour of every day.

It made me feel so grateful that my mam would be making the long journey especially to see me.

Visiting day arrived and I ran eagerly into the welcoming arms of my mam. She had lots of news for me about events back home, and showed me a recent photograph of my sister, who had grown since I had last seen her. She said they

83

had sent something to Santa Claus and that they felt sure I would like, and he would be delivering it on Christmas Eve. She also reminded me That I would be having a medical early in the new year and that if they received a letter saying I was to be discharged, then she would sign her letter from '*Dad and Mam*,' instead of '*Mam and and Dad*.' She knew the letters were read before being given to patients, so I was to watch for the alteration when the time came.

At 2.30 p.m. Sister Devereaux and Miss Moran entered the dining room.

Then it was the time for all our rehearsals to bear fruit and for us to sing our rendition.

Sister called for everyone's attention.

"The children have a seasonal surprise," she said.

Miss Moran seated herself at the piano, and we all stood beside the fireplace and in a well rehearsed formation. Miss Moran played the opening chords and then we sang '*Silent Night*.'

Every single verse we sang perfectly. Not one girl made even the slightest mistake, while the descant added an enchantment to that plaintive carol.

After the singing was over we stood with our heads bowed and there fell upon the dining room a poignant silence, almost as if we had mesmerised our audience. Then after a few seconds the silence was destroyed by a rapturous applause.

We raised our heads and we saw all of the mothers had tears running down their cheeks, while fathers were wiping their eyes and blowing their noses. It was without doubt an musical interlude never to be forgotten by either the children or their parents.

Mam hugged and kissed me, saying how proud she was of me and said she could not wait to tell Daddy all about it when she got home.

What a magical visiting day this had turned out to be.

Sister Devereaux stood smiling by the door and was wishing the parents a Happy Christmas as they left the room.

Chapter 15.

Art lessons in the school room saw us painting
Christmas cards to send home to our families, and I was
taking extra care with mine. I wanted to convey just how
much I loved everyone back home.

My days no longer seemed boring.

There was so much going on.

Matron one morning surprised us all by making one of
her rare visits to the dining room. She informed us that every
year the children in the hospital staged a nativity play, and
that a cross section of children from all four sections of the
hospital would be selected to take part. Members of the
public would be allowed into the schoolroom for a small fee
to watch the performance, and money raised would go to the
hospital funds allocated to treats.

When Matron had left we were all speculating as to who
in our section would be chosen for this auspicious occasion. I
hoped if I were selected I would play the Virgin Mary.

A few days later Christine and I learned that we had
been chosen to play the part of angels, along with two more
of Sister Devereaux's patients. It was not the role I had
hoped for, but given the number of places available Christine
and I were quite privileged even to be taking part.

As for the rehearsals for the nativity play I found them
quite irksome, for we found it quite hard to communicate
with girls and boys from other wards. Christine and I, plus
two other Fortitude patients were angels, kept mostly to
ourselves on account of the other patients not properly
accepting us. The rest of the cast had split off into groups
from their respective wards, becoming suspicious of all
others.

After observing them over the coming days I found
myself yet again having kind thoughts about Sister
Devereaux, for she insisted on good manners and respectful
attitudes being uppermost amongst her girls. These clinging

cliques would never have been tolerated had Sister been here.

The day came of the opening came a photographer came to take our photographs, followed by the arrival of the general public who paid to enter the schoolroom and to watch the nativity play. We had to put on two performances to meet demand, such was the number of people wanting to buy tickets.

The photographs were available for parents to purchase, but it was an expense that most parents could not afford.

The nativity play coincided with a number of seasonal changes to the routine. For instance when I was admitted the only time I had heard the piano being played was when the day shift nurses sang their evening hymns before going off duty. Now however, in the run up to Christmas, we were getting little treats, for a young doctor who could play very well had started popping his his head round the dining room door. He would smile brightly at us all and then wanted to know if he should play for us.

We always answered with a resounding:

"Yes please!"

He was a jolly man though in a somewhat academic way, though full of seasonal good will. He would bounce into the room, full of energy and zest. With his stethoscope hanging around his neck he would seat himself at the piano and would play Christmas Carols or a medley of tunes to which we could all sing along.

Before leaving he would always approach the desk and would stand quietly chatting with Sister Devereaux, but we noticed he would never stop and talk with Staff Nurse Briggs when she was deputising for Sister. On those occasions he was absent. Unfortunately the doctor's visits ceased closer to Christmas and he never returned. Our musical treats were at an end.

When December 24th dawned I awoke in high spirits knowing it was Christmas Eve. Even the hated coughing and spitting did not seem as irksome as it usually did. It felt like there was magic in he air as we went through our daily routine in the washroom and the dining room.

The sky was dark with pattering rain on the windowpanes. Sister Devereaux decided that perhaps a short walk around the streets would be preferable on a such a wet morning, so with thin waterproof jackets over our coats we set off.

Everyone was chattering about what they hoped Santa would bring them, and at first I was joining in, until I began to notice the preparations in the houses we were passing. Regularly I saw a house with either trimmings or a Christmas tree visible through its windows, and inevitably I began to think of home. Mam and dad would have put up the artificial tree that they brought out every year, and I wondered who had trimmed it up, since it had been my job for as long as I could remember. I would hang the bells and baubles on the branches and then draw a star that I would place on the top.

I noticed in one of the houses that two little girls were looking out through a bedecked window whilst behind them stood their mother. The sight stabbed home like a dagger and my earlier mood of high elation evaporated. I was enveloped by a dark melancholia. I so desperately wanted to be at home with family again. I wanted to be like those two girls, with my mother attending us.

Christine soon sensed that I was not my normal self.

"Eleanor, what is wrong?"

"I want to be at home," I said.

"Well I miss home too," she said in a pained way. "And I am just the same as you," she said, "I have never spent a Christmas away from my family."

She continued explaining our predicament but I was not listening, for I had slipped deep down into a sombre mood that was so full of self-pity that I could not pull myself out of it.

Christine eventually turned her attention to Flora and Ann, having made no progress with me whilst I walked in a miserable silence.

When we arrived back at the hospital the trimmings that I had so enthusiastically helped to make seemed meaningless now. When the midday meal was served I ate with head bowed, not wishing to talk with anyone.

We had begun to leave the dining room for the thirty minutes lying on our beds following our meal, but when I reached the door Sister Devereaux barred my way and gently drew me to her side. We waited until the dining room was empty and then she walked me over to her desk. She then drew up a chair alongside her own for me to sit on.

"What is the matter with you?" she asked.

"Nothing, Sister," I replied.

"Don't you lie to me," she responded sharply. "I will ask you once again. What is the matter?"

I did not answer at firstly because I did not know how to put into words exactly how I was feeling. Secondly, even if I had been capable of expressing how I felt, Sister would have been the last person I would have confided in..

"Are you not going to tell me what is troubling you?" she asked.

I looked up at her expecting to see a stern expression but was surprised to see her features were soft and that she had concern in her eyes. When she took my hand in hers and then smiled I found myself beginning to tell her my thoughts.

At first I spoke hesitantly and then it all came tumbling out.

"When I was walking I saw children - the children in their real homes," I added before revealing my gloomiest face. "I want to be home with my mam and dad and not here in the hospital."

I continued with a lengthy explanation about how I had seen seen Christmas trees and trimmings through the windows of houses, but that worst of all I was seeing happy families.

"I wish that was me," I said,

When I finally fell silent she addressed me.

"You are not alone here, Eleanor," she began. "Just about every child in this hospital is the experiencing the same emotions. This is why I am making every effort to try to ensure that all of my girls enjoy the festive season, despite being away from their loved ones. Everything that can be done is being done just as far as funds will allow. Are you not going to reach out and accept the joy and happiness I am striving to give you?"

She sat still and awaited my response and then added:

"Or am I wasting my time?"

Her last few words jolted me into realising that despite her strictness with us all, she was nevertheless doing her best.

She watched me.

"Well are you going to reach out?"

"Yes, Sister," I replied whilst trying to smile, "I am going to enjoy Christmas."

"Good, I am pleased," she said, smiling, and then glancing at her watch she said:

"Oh look," she said with her usual rigour, "it will soon be time for school."

I stared at Sister in complete surprise.

"But nobody goes to school on Christmas Even," I said.

Then seeing she perhaps had not heard me, I plucked up the courage and said:

"But it is a school holiday, Sister."

"Is it?" she said, raising an eyebrow. "Well not today I'm afraid."

She walked over to the windows overlooking Fortitude Ward and tapped and signalled the girls to rise and to return to the dining room.

When they were all assembled she addressed us all.

"Right girls. Time for school," she announced. "Come on, make haste!"

There were groans all round, with mumblings of it being unfair, but no one questioned her instruction.

Everyone slowly made their way down the corridor , through Courtesy Ward and into the schoolroom.

What we saw there made us gasp with amazement.

Seated at the far end of the room and on the platform we had used for the nativity play was Santa Claus.

Piled beside that happy figure was a large pile of Christmas parcels, each with a nametag on it.

Chairs had been arranged around the room so that all of us could be seated. Then Santa began to pick up parcels and read out the names, whilst nurses with tinsel bows tied to their aprons arrived and were helping Santa distribute his gifts.

Sister was stood near the door, thoroughly enjoying watching our surprised reactions.

When my turn came I was handed a large oblong parcel, which I eagerly unwrapped, revealing a Post Office set. Inside were tiny envelopes and miniature sheets of writing-paper. There was a cut-out post office with instructions to 'fold along the dotted lines' and then there flaps to fold and insert into slots to hold it cardboard model in place. There was also a cut-out post box that assembled in the same way with the same way. Tiny postage stamps and a little rubber stamp was there for franking the mail and dispatching. Finally there was a board with a flat picture of an avenue with numbered houses on it.

I was absolutely delighted and my dark thoughts were completely dispelled. Sister Devereaux was right, It was up to me to enjoy everything the hospital was offering during this festive time.

Christine was uppermost in my mind, for she too was missing home, but I had been so wrapped up in myself that I had not even listened to what she had been saying. I should have done, for she had been feeling as homesick too. I decided to apologise to her at the earliest opportunity. This was something new for me, for I could not recall ever in my life having made an apology to a friend before.

She smiled.

"I do understand, Eleanor" she said. "You need not apologise."

I experienced a warm glow within my heart, having learnt that it pays to be open and admitting to being wrong as often as possible When we went to bed on Christmas Eve the excitement in Fortitude Ward was at its absolute height, and it took us quite some time to finally drop off to sleep. We having prepared for Christmas as well as anyone.

Chapter 16.

The next morning we were awake even before the night nurse arrived with the coughing bowls and we were eagerly looking under our beds. Sure enough under my bed there were some presents. I leaned over and pulled them all up onto the bed and frantically began to open mine. The first one was from my mam and dad and it was a beautiful pot doll. My mam, who was good at sewing, had made its clothes from scraps of material from dresses that my sister had grown out of. The doll even had little shoes on her feet.

Oh how I loved her!

There were other presents from my aunties and uncles and from the neighbours who remembered me fondly.

The laughter and joy of happy children in the ward was deafening and the night nurse and Sister Kirshaw were stood with smiling faces, enjoying the happy scene. There was no walk that morning. All anyone wanted to do was play with their toys. For once Sister did not chide us for making too much noise and it seemed we could do anything we liked that morning within reason. Sister was obviously enjoying seeing us all so happy.

I felt sorry for the nursing staff that had to work on Christmas Day. Surely they would have preferred to be at home enjoying the festivities with their families? Yet I noticed that nurses Mollett and Stubbs seemed especially happy, as did Sister Devereaux. If they resented being there they were certainly not showing it.

At 11.30 we were instructed to put all of our new toys into our bedside lockers, and then line up in the dining room for inspection. Sister walked down the line of girls to make sure we were all presentable, then we set off on a walk for the full length of the main corridor.

Although I had walked down this corridor several times I still never ceased to wonder at just how large the hospital must be. There were so many sections, each divided by fire doors, and every section had doors to either side - so many of them closed and mysterious. I could not begin to think how many rooms there must be in total, and this was only the ground floor. Then when one looked at the hospital from the outside one could be spires and domes, so what if there were mysterious rooms in those too?

I voiced my thoughts to Christine and we had the most breathtaking conversation about what it would be like to be lost in this place in the dead of night without a person around. Our imaginations ran away with us, as we considered how many ghosts and ghouls would have us at their mercy without our dutiful nurses to save us. We were laughing and giggling all of the way down the corridor until at last we reached the concert room but where our scatty conversations were halted.

In that room there was a wonderful sight to behold, for at one side of the stage there stood a huge Chrstmas tree towering towards the ceiling and the tree was laden with trimmings and many children's drawings of angels and other festive themes. Festoons of colourful paper chains and balloons were pinned to the ceiling and the walls, as were clumps of mistletoe swaying and twirling. There were also tinseled angels on ribbons and short banners with Santa's happy face and the words 'Merry Christmas' reading down them.

Trestle tables had been set up with fancy tablecloths and with a Christmas cracker at every place. In the middle of each trestle table was stood a card with the name of a ward written on it, so we quickly found Fortitude Ward and took our places, though then fidgeting with anticipation.

Matron entered the room and called for quiet, and we all had to close our eyes while she said an appropriate prayer. Then whilst the dinner was being served we pulled our crackers and had paper hats to put on our heads.

It was a wonderful traditional Christmas dinner, in fact the best I could ever remember.

My mam always did her best, but with food rationing causing so much misery she found it difficult sometimes to cook anything special. Her baking-day had been reduced to once a month because she did not have enough lard for luxuries of the kind that I ate that day. I marvelled at how the hospital had managed to put on such a feast, for after our turkey dinner we had Christmas pudding and custard and then platefuls of mince pies were brought to every table. I could not remembering seeing so much food and I ate until I felt I would burst.

How happy we all were!

I looked around the room and saw all of the nursing staff sitting together and enjoying their Christmas dinner too.

Then everybody's heads were quickly turned towards the stage when the tune "*Jingle Bells*' was playing was muffled as if the sound was coming from back stage. The curtains moved slightly, causing a hush in the room then everyone waited.

The curtains were drawn back and Santa Claus was revealed in all his merriment carrying sacks overflowing with presents.

"*Ho! Ho! Ho! Merry Christmas!*" he said and we all shouted back at the tops of our voices:

"*Happy Christmas Santa!*"

He then distributed presents by reading out our names.

Children who were able-bodied went up the steps onto the stage, whilst nurses collected the gifts for those who were in wheelchairs.

Then just as we thought that it could not get any better, staff cleared the tables of cutlery and basins and plates and then the trestle-tables were moved away. The chairs were set in rows and a silver screen was dropped down above the stage and a film projector was brought. The curtains were then drawn across the windows, the lights were dimmed, and one of the doctors announced that we were to watch a Western.

He had to pause until the boys had stopped cheering, and then explained, as most of us knew, that the good characters would be dressed in white and the bad characters would be dressed in black, (since those were the codes of the movies in those days). It was our right to cheer "Hooray!" for the appearance of a good characters and shout a firm "Boo!" for the bad ones.

The euphoria we shared in that concert hall was magical and was the best tonic for those that were homesick. At the end of that long day eighteen happy girls lay in their beds in Fortitude Ward, with no means to resist the effects of such comforts as we had received and that would send us to sleep.

Then on December 27th my dad came to visit me for the first time. I was so happy to hug and kiss him again. I was amazed at the difference in him, for as my mam had said he no longer needed the crutches. Instead he was wearing one surgical shoe with a thick sole. He walked into the dining room erect and looking every inch of his six feet in height.

He had come prepared with some entertainment for me and had me amazed and giggling at his magic tricks. He said everyone had missed me back home on Christmas Day and they would be pleased that I liked my new doll. He said also that everyone at home were keeping their fingers crossed that I would be discharged after the medical on January 5th.

"What a wonderful start to 1948 it would be to have our family reunited again!" he said.

I told him how homesick I sometimes felt, and he replied with one of his stories.

"I know exactly what you mean," he said. "When I was in the army during the war I was allowed home only for very important occasions. I was back home for your baby sister's christening. But for all the time that I was away I had photographs of you all that I kept here in my wallet," he said. "All I could think about was what you think about, which is going home one day, but sooner I am sure than I did."

It was so comforting to know that Dad really did know how I felt.

All too soon that visit was over and as he kissed me goodbye he dabbed my tears away with his handkerchief. I stood at the dining room window and when I could see him waved to him until he disappeared from view.

Chapter 17.

Every girl was tense on the day of the January 1948 medicals. Christine, who had now been in the hospital for nine months, was especially optimistic, feeling sure that her big day was near. I hoped that if she was discharged then I too would be going home, because I could not imagine what my days would be like in the hospital without her.

Our usual morning walk was cancelled and instead, following breakfast, girls from Fortitude Ward hastened into the washroom and began frantically coughing into the toilets and wash basins. We were all hoping that if we cleared our lungs so that we did not wheeze or rattle then the doctor might consider us cured.

Medicals commenced. I was weighed, and to my disappointment I had lost three pounds since being admitted. How could I have lost three pounds when I had been eating so well? The doctor examined me closely, and try as I might I could not control the wheezing in my chest. I came out of the examination room with a heavy heart.

Christine was more optimistic, for her weight had not changed, and she felt certain she was breathing easier than ever. Flora was in high spirits. She was positive that she would be going home, for she had gained weight, and she said the doctor looked pleased as he examined her.

Over a week passed, during which time I was carefully checking how my mother finished off her letters, looking for her signing off with '*from Mam and Dad*,' but I watched in vain.

Ten days later, the names of the girls who were to be discharged were announced. Six Courtesy Ward girls were going home, as were three of the five Patience Ward girls, but only two girls in Fortitude Ward were to be discharged, namely Connie, who had been in the hospital for over a year, and Flora's best friend Anne. My name was not read out and I was bitterly disappointed, and even though I had tried not to build up my hopes, I could not suppress my tears.

Christine was extremely upset and try as I might I could not find the words to console her. Flora however, to my surprise, was worse than either of us. She had been so certain that she would be discharged, and it made my heart grieve to see this usually cheerful girl so downcast. All her zest and high spiritedness had deserted her. The fact that her best friend had been discharged did not help matters either. I tried to talk to Flora but she pushed me away, telling me to leave her alone.

Meanwhile Dorothy, who seemed always to be homesick, was inconsolable.

Our morning walk, as I say, was cancelled. Instead, those of us who had not been discharged had to form a queue outside the dining room to be be counselled by Sister Devereaux or a nurse. I was hoping that I would not get Sister, for although I no longer disliked her, I nevertheless felt ill at ease whenever I was alone with her.

I was fortunate, for it was Nurse Owens who talked to me. I put my arms around her neck whilst she kissed and hugged me, something I could never have done with Sister Devereaux. Nurse Owens waited until my tears abated, then she explained matters to me.

"The illness you are suffering from can rarely be cured in a mere twelve weeks, Eleanor, but I can tell you that the doctors are satisfied with your progress."

I slumped a little.

"My mam and dad told me they were sure I would be back with them in the New Year," I said with a gathering disbelief.

Nurse Owens wrote this down in book.

"I am writing that down, it is purely routine."

I was to learn later that a cautionary letter was written by Sister Devereaux to my parents asking them to refrain from building up my hopes of being discharged, as this was considered detrimental to recovery.

When the counselling was over I sat quietly thinking about what Nurse Owens had said, and wondering how I would get through another twelve weeks here, especially as I was missing my family more than ever.

Then where I was sat in the dining room I overheard Nurse Owens talking to Nurse Mollett, and which interrupted my thoughts.

Nurse Owens was complaining that two and a half years after the war everything was still being rationed.

"I just so fed up of shortages, especially the clothes, I have so many things I have to repair, " she said.

Then Sister Devereaux joined the conversation and commented on rations during the war itself.

This was why the nurses were always looking at fashion magazines. They stared with envy at models wearing the latest Paris fashions, because the rationing of clothing did not run to anything designed in Paris.

I returned to my thoughts when I had first arrived, that the young nurses were no different from the young people at home. The restrictions stretched across the country and beyond. It was a time of waiting, just as I waited, and my own waiting merged into the lives of others.

Chapter 18.

During the following week many changes took place, New patients being admitted replaced the number of girls returning home, and in some cases brought disruption to close-knit friendships. Each time a new patient was admitted and had gone though all the preliminaries, we all felt a deep empathy with how she was feeling when Sister Devereaux introduced her to us and while the new patient stood with her head lowered.

I briefly saw one patient who was presented in the dining room who was to be a patient in Courtesy Ward. Although I knew it was rude to stare, I could not take my eyes off her. A nurse walked either side of her as she tried to walk. Her legs moving jerkily and were being flung out of step as she walked and made it almost impossible for her to support herself. The nurses held her arms steady but her hands were trembling and shaking and she was clenching and unclenching her fingers. What affected me most however was her face, for she was making the most grotesque expressions imaginable as she screwed her eyes up as tight as she could and then opening them wide, which altogether was like some mediaeval representation of insanity.

I was deeply affected by the sight of her, and I wished I could remove the memory from my mind, for it was like a living nightmare I had witnessed.

I later asked Nurse Mollett what what was wrong with her.

"She has Chorea, Eleanor, or St Vitus Dance as it used to be called," she said. "It is common to find it among children who were down in the shelters during the air-raids and who could not cope with it. The shaking eventually gets worse."

Then Nurse Mollett put a hand on my shoulder.

"But you must not worry, with our help she will soon be well again."

As for my own ward there were two vacant beds in Fortitude Ward, and one of the new girls turned out to be as selfish and anti-social as they come. Her name was Rebecca Roberts. She was 10 years old with light brown hair and blue eyes. It was soon apparent that she came from a home where her parents had indulged her every whim, for she did not intend anyone to even breath on let alone touch any of her possessions. We all sat on the bench in order of height. On the right was Flora, and on my left was Christine. Rebecca when she sat down was placed on Christine's left, and so was next but one to me.

My mam wrote regularly to me, and very occasionally I would receive a parcel with some crayons and a colouring book, or else some comics to read. Rebecca however received parcels so frequently that I do not remember a girl who received so much. Whatever she received however was hers and hers alone. If another girl as much as looked at her comics then Rebecca would become very bad-tempered and would speak sharply to them. We had seen Sister Devereaux on many occasions calling Rebecca to her desk and talking to her, and each time Rebecca would stand with a sulky face, obviously not liking what she was hearing. Nurse Owens and Nurse Mollett also spend time talking to Rebecca, but nothing either of them said seemed to make the slightest bit of difference.

Christine, unfortunately, was sat next to Rebecca at the dining table and although she tried to be friendly with Rebecca she did not succeed. Rebecca gave us all the impression that she considered herself better than all of us, and no one liked her attitude at all. Flora had not even tried to befriend Rebecca, even though her best friend, Anne, had gone home. Flora was missing Anne, but she nevertheless enjoyed playing with Christine and I, and we became a happy trio.

Flora was very vocal about Rebecca.

"She is a stuck-up selfish little prig,' Flora explained. "Just because her fancy Mummy and Daddy can afford to send her expensive presents does not mean she can lord it over us," she said.

In the meantime Sister's patience was running thin, so when one playtime Rebecca let out a peevish squeal as someone touched one of her toys, Sister Devereaux sharply demanded that she approach her desk.Sister reprimanded her in front of everyone and required Rebecca to stand with her hands on her head and her eyes closed and facing everyone in the room until Sister gave the order that she could be at ease. For ten long ten long minutes Rebecca stood there. We could see from her posture that her arms were beginning to ache, and the relief on her face was apparent when Sister told her to return to her seat.

Rebecca sat down next to Christine, her face screwed up with emotion, and displayed an emerging hatred of Sister Devereaux. How deep this hatred was we could not discover because Rebecca refused to talk to us. Rebecca had created an unpleasant atmosphere, and we were all hoping that Sister Devereaux's stern words, plus the humiliation, would put an end to the problem.

The following day as we headed for the schoolroom for our morning lesson my thoughts returned to the girl who had been admitted with Chorea, and I decided to look for her as we walked through Courtesy Ward.

I spotted her immediately, since the other eight beds were unoccupied. What I saw filled me with terror.

The girl was laid in bed on her back with the sides of the bed raised where two leather belts were attached and had been stretched tight across her. One strap was across her chest and the other was across her legs. Her arms were flailing around, her face was contorting and she was moaning in misery. For a second or two I thought I was visiting a torture chamber. I walked up to her bed and I smiled at her but could not respond, in fact I doubted that she could even speak.

I found my hour in the schoolroom extremely tedious, for my thoughts were with that poor girl.

How I wished that I could help her.

Meanwhile the problem with Rebecca was still ongoing. We had all thought Sister's stern words, and the humiliation she had suffered would have put an end to the problem. However to our surprise Rebecca still persisted in her anti-social behaviour, for very soon she was causing trouble again, but this time not only to herself, but also for Christine.

Following mealtime and in the dining room Rebecca discovered she had misplaced her handkerchief, and planned to take one from someone else when they were not looking. Sister had gone down to Courtesy Ward and only Nurse Owens was in the room. Standing behind Christine, Rebecca carefully pulled Christine's handkerchief out from her pocket.

Christine would not have been any the wiser if Flora had not seen her do it. Flora told me and then we both told Christine what Rebecca had done,

Upon checking her pocket, and finding her hankie was missing, Christine yelled at Rebecca.

"Give it back!" she shouted.

Rebecca assumed an innocent look.

"I do not know what you are talking about, it wasn't me that stole your hankie!" Rebecca shouted back.

Flora joined in the argument.

"But I saw you take it! You have to give it back to Christine!" Flora yelled just as loudly.

Rebecca stamped her foot.

"But this is my hankie!" she said defiantly to Christine. "It is that girl there," said Rebecca, who pointed at Flora, "who is a stupid liar!" she shouted.

This last remark made Flora see red, and before Rebecca even realised what was happening Flora had lurched at Rebecca and grabbed a handful of her hair and was pulling it as hard as she could.

Rebecca rolled her head to alleviate the drag on her scalp and at the same time reached out and dug her nails into Flora's cheek.

Flora let out a yell and pulled even harder, whilst Christine and I were trying to separate them.

Nurse Owens came over immediately and dragged them apart, and a second later Sister Devereaux walked through the door, and upon realising what was happening she ordered the four of us to stand before her desk whilst the rest of the girls in the dining room looked on.

"I will not tolerate such appalling behaviour," Sister said who was looking sternly at all four of us.

"Who instigated this?"

"She did," said Rebecca while pointing at Christine, "she said I stole her hankie."

"And did you?" asked Sister sternly.

"No, I did not," replied Rebecca.

"Yes you did, you liar!" snapped Flora.

"Quiet, all of you," said Sister. "I need to speak to each of you one at a time."

Then she seated herself behind her desk.

"Eadie, Hastings and Wilson, stand over there facing me, and no talking. Roberts, remain where you are," she said.

We did as we were told.

All the other girls began talking amongst themselves, their interest in the affair waning, whilst Flora, Christine and I watched Rebecca intently. We could not hear one word Sister said, for she spoke so quietly, but we could hear Rebecca protesting her innocence.

Rebecca then returned to her seat, her face dark with anger and obviously not happy with what Sister had said to her. She sat scowling with her arms folded.

Next it was Flora, then Christine, and then finally me.

I told Sister exactly what had witnessed and what had been said and done. She listened quietly and then she told me to sit down.

A couple of minutes later she summoned us all to her desk again and there was a hush in the room as the rest of the girls listened.

"Flora Wilson," she said. "Are you fully aware that I do not tolerate violence amongst girls, regardless of the provocation? There are more civilised ways to settle a dispute without resorting to fighting. You will therefore go to bed at six o' clock for two nights, beginning this evening."

Then she looked Christine and I.

Hastings and Eadie. In future you will not take matters into your own hands, but approach me instead. I am always ready to listen and hopefully settle disputes amicably."

Sister then turned to Rebecca.

"Roberts," she said. "Your behaviour has been atrocious from the moment you entered this hospital. You have no consideration for anyone except yourself. Not only are you selfish, but now I find that you are not averse to telling lies. This has got to stop - NOW!" she demanded, whilst pointing a forefinger and looking sternly at Rebecca.

"You will go to bed at six o' clock every evening forthwith until such time as I consider you have learned the error of your ways."

What happened next not only amazed us, it also took Sister by surprise.

Rebecca had a temper tantrum, right there in front of Sister's desk. She screamed and stamped her feet and her face was contorted with anger.

"I despise you!" she screamed, seeming to spit out the words. "Also I absolutely refused to go to bed early. You have turned this hospital into a prison, It is an awful place and I hate it!"

Rebecca would have said more had Sister Devereaux not stood up and walked over to rebecca and slapped her hard on the cheek.

Rebecca was so shocked by this unexpected action that she stopped screaming and stamping and began sobbing pitifully.

Sister Devereaux then took Rebecca's hand and led her out of the dining-room.

I had never known the dining room so quiet, for never had we seen anything like this before. Then slowly we all began to discuss what we had witnessed in hushed tones, as if even now Sister Devereaux could hear us.

Christine was solemn.

"I feel terrible, Flora, that you are to be punished for defending me," she said with shame.

"No," said Flora, "it was rebecca's fault, not yours or mine."

Staff Nurse Briggs took over Sister's duty and we did not see Sister Devereaux again that day, apart from when the day shift sang their hymns prior to leaving.

Rebecca's bed in Fortitude Ward was empty. Christine and Flora and I wondered what had happened to her.

Where had Sister taken her?

Flora obliged with her own suspicion.

"Perhaps she has been locked up - behind the forbidden door," she said.

We all fell silent at the thought of this.

Just what had happened to Rebecca? We all marvelled at her nerve, since whenever we were stood before Sister Devereaux when she was cross we had hardly dared breathe, let alone utter a single word of defiance.

Christine considered the matter.

"Screaming like that is probably how Rebecca gets her own way at home," she said. "Rebecca must have thought it would here just as easily."

Flora agreed.

"I don't like that girl one little bit, but what she said was everything I wanted to say and more besides," she said.

Christine pondered this.

"Does that mean you want to be friends with Rebecca?" Christine asked.

Flora replied with mixed feelings.

"I do not think Rebecca will make a single friend in this hospital," said Flora who was dabbing at her cheek, "but - by hell - she is the bravest girl we have had and I think every girl will want to know more about her."

Christine, ever the judge in contentious matters, spoke next.

"Flora is right," she said. "We cannot really make a friend of Rebecca, but we cannot ignore her either. Even if she does not like any of us Rebecca is going to drag us all into more trouble again unless we do something about it."

Then Christine reminded us of our duty.

"Sister will get very sour if girls are not friendly to each other."

Then she shrugged her shoulder and looked away.

"But to do anything at all we first need to know where Rebecca is."

When Sister Kilshaw came into the ward for her nightly inspection then one of the girls asked her why Rebecca was not in her bed.

Sister Kilshaw looked at us over the tops of her glasses and began to stammer so much that we all knew she was ill at ease. There were then many ums and errs, until eventually she spoke,

"I am sure I am n-n- not allowed to say where that girl has been taken," she said. Then she hastily made for the door.

"You should all of you -g-go to sleep," she said. "Goodnight and God Bless," she said after.

The mystery had deepened, and as I lay in bed I could hear the soft whispers of girls talking to each other, no doubt speculating on the fate that Rebecca had suffered at the hands of Sister Devereaux.

Chapter 19.

When we awoke the following morning Rebecca's bed was still unoccupied. Then for five long days we waited and wondered. Over those five days staff never mentioned her name. When we asked nurses directly then they replied that they knew nothing.

Rebecca became the topic of many conversations. There had on occasion been times when a girl had 'disappeared,' but it had always been announced shortly after that the girl had gone home and had been unable to say goodbye to everyone.

No such announcement had been made about Rebecca.

Then information began to seep through from the girls who were shoe cleaners, who had allegedly overheard some nurses outside talking about Rebecca. Gossip began to circulate amongst us all in the manner of the game 'Chinese Whispers.' One shoe cleaner said she had heard a nurse talking about Rebecca having personal behaviour problems, and another nurse had felt sorry for her, given the circumstances. When we heard this we could not understand how anyone could feel sorry for Rebecca, because we did not like her. Then various rumours began to circulate, the most exciting one being that Rebecca had been locked behind the Forbidden Door, which was a rumour that held everyone's attention.

Then on the morning that was six days after Rebecca's disappearance we were surprised to see that Rebecca was sitting on a chair next to Sister Devereaux's desk. Her hair had been groomed, and her head was bowed. Her eyes were fixed on her hands and her fingers fidgeted nervously.

We could not wait to see what was going to happen next.

As was the usual routine we had our temperature checked and our medication administered and our hair combed

Then while we were all seated at our tables awaiting breakfast Sister Devereaux called for our attention.

She indicated to Rebecca that she should stand up. Rebecca obeyed immediately, though with downcast eyes and hands clasped together.

Everyone in the room was silent.

Then Sister spoke.

"Rebecca, I believe you have something to say to everyone."

Rebecca remained silent, wringing her hands.

Sister Devereaux began to rise from her seat, at which Rebecca immediately began to speak.

"I want to apologise," she blurted out, and then she paused and turned to look at Sister and then continued, "for my anti-social behaviour."

Sister, who had sat down again, spoke again.

"Rebecca, turn around."

Rebecca turned around to face Sister Devereaux,

Then to our absolute surprise Flora, Christine and I were summoned to approach the desk too.

We all anxiously obeyed and then Sister addressed us.

"I want you all to apologise to each other, regardless of whether you feel an apology is due."

We all stood still.

"Well, come along," Sister said, "I am waiting."

Christine made the first move, apologising to each of us. Then Flora did the same, and so did I. Finally Rebecca made her apologies.

"I want no ill-feeling between you, " Sister said sternly. "Any more problems and you are to come and see me. Understood?"

"Yes, Sister," we replied together.

"That is all," she said. You may now return to your seats."

When the four of us were sat down we immediately began to talking to Rebecca, for we felt sorry that she had undergone such an awful ordeal. Her eyes were red from crying, but she nevertheless managed a smile in response to our coaxing. We all wanted to know where she had been for the past few days.

"I was in another part of the hospital," she said.

Then our questions took us no further and she in her turn was reluctant to tell us anything more.

Thus a truce was shared between us, albeit one imposed by Sister Devereaux.

Flora, ever the dramatic soul, began talking to Rebecca regularly to satisfy her curiosity as to Rebecca's unusual personality. Christine made a great effort to be friendly with her, though I myself did not posses the tact, diplomacy and insight that Christine had. We also kept noticing Sister Devereaux taking Rebecca to one side to have further talks with her.

Rebecca had now become a more subdued girl, and just a week later Flora was astonished when rebecca, who had received yet another parcel from home, passed Flora a comic.

"Would you like to borrow this?" she asked.

"Thank you," said Flora in a surprised tone, and then smiled.

This in turn caused Rebecca to smile, and then Rebecca also distributed comics to Christine and I.

Over the weeks that followed our friendship with Rebecca flourished, The spoilt child had disappeared and was replaced by a much happier and friendlier girl who no longer coveted her possessions and readily shared her many books and toys. Even more surprising was Flora and Rebecca becoming best friends. Their beds were placed together and as playmates they became inseparable. Our previous little trio of friends became a foursome enjoying our days together.

The dramatic arrival of Rebecca had helped to dispel my gloom following the decision of the doctors to not discharge me, and I found that I began to settle down in the hospital.

Over the ensuing months Rebecca revealed a couple of snippets of information about her home life. One was that she lived with her grandparents, who loved her dearly, and that she did not have a daddy because her mother was not married. Secondly she had been the victim of bullying at school, where other children had called her a *'bastard child.'* None of the rest of us knew exactly what this meant, but in later years I appreciated the hurt the taunting must have caused.

In the 1930's to have a child out of wedlock was considered shameful, the mother was classed as a *'fallen woman,'* and the innocent child was subject to appalling treatment.

Also I should say that every time I walked through Courtesy War I looked for the Chorea girl and found her improvement was rapid. Just three months later that very same girl walked into the dining room to say goodbye to us all, and she did so without the slightest twitch or tremor. I felt such a surge of admiration for the skills of the doctors and nursing staff.

I was to see many more patients suffering from Chorea, and the sight became commonplace for me. They no longer distressed me, knowing as I did that they would make a full recovery.

Chapter 19.

One Saturday morning following breakfast Sister made an announcement.

"Thanks to all the kind people who have donated money to the hospital we are to have a special treat," she said,

Every child in that dining room seemed breathlessly quiet, waiting to hear what the treat might be.

Sister continued.

"The film '*Lassie Come Home,*" is showing at the cinema in Hoylake. Would you all like to go and see it?"

The noise of children shouting: "*Yes please!*" was deafening.

Sister waited until the cries had abated before continuing.

"Our trip is scheduled for this afternoon, immediately following your midday meal," she said.

We were all tense with excitement, especially as it was a Lassie film, and according to the frantic information being passed around, the film would be in technicolour.

Before I entered the hospital, a trip to the cinema had been a very rare event for me. My parents could not often afford such luxuries. It was 1950 before I began going to the cinema on a regular basis and became familiar with the film stars.

The walk that morning was to Heather Hill, but we all seemed oblivious to our surroundings. It was as if we were walking in sleep, for our minds were fixed on on our forthcoming trip to pictures.

Even unhappy Dorothy was smiling.

When finally we stood waiting for the bus there was escalating excitement, especially as many of us had not travelled by bus for a long time. It was a short journey to Hoylake and very soon we were walking towards the cinema.

So many time back home I had walked past a cinema and looked enviously at the people queuing to get in. This time however I would be in the queue.

In big letters above the entrance was the title '*Lassie Come Home*,' with a picture of the famous Collie dog in full colour in the poster-windows beneath. I looked at the stills from the movie as we moved slowly up the queue, then when we reached the door Nurse Owens bought our tickets at the kiosk and then all of us entered.

Warm air flooded over me as we walked across the foyer whilst I felt the deep carpeting beneath my feet. There were no carpeted floors in the hospital.

In the cinema there was soft lighting and in those days also, the persistent smell of cigarette smoke. An usherette led us to our seats near the front where we all sat together on the same row, with a nurse at each end. Christine, Flora, Rebecca and I were set together with Nurse Owens sitting on the end next to Christine.

The ceiling and walls of the cinema were ornately decorated and on looking behind me I saw people were continued to stream in through the black doors. Soon the cinema was resounding with the noise of people happily chatting to one another. There were lots of children accompanied by adults. The children were dressed in so many playful cheerful colours and not uniforms of navy blue. They would be returning to their homes that evening. No sleeping outdoors for them.

In addition to the cigarette smoke there was a profusion of perfumes and I wondered if we should be noticed, since the smell of carbolic was clinging to our hair, clothes and bodies.

Then a dimming of the lights interrupted my thoughts. The curtains drew back. And from that moment on we were all spellbound.

We watched a Laurel and Hardy short, and then a cartoon, followed by Pathe News, which I little understood apart from news of the King and Queen.

The curtains closed, the lights came back on and an usherette appeared with a tray full of ice-creams and drinks. Children began leaving their seats and forming a queue. We wanted an ice-cream too, but the nurses said they did not have any money left. I could barely watch those children carrying their ice-creams, I was so envious.

Ice-creams were forgotten however when once again the curtains opened, and in glorious Technicolour came the title for '*Lassie Come Home.*'

I had not seen a Lassie film before because I had always felt nervous around dogs. However I found myself adoring Lassie with her antics and then her long and desperate trek to return to her owners. I kept shedding a tear and towards the end we were all snivelling into our hankies.

It was at this point that Christine nudged me with her elbow. I ignored her but then she nudged me again more forcefully. When I had dragged my eyes away from the screen I was instructed to look at Nurse Owens, who had tears cascading down her cheeks by the bucketful.

We all came out of the cinema extremely happy, and we accepted as a troupe that every one of us girls had been crying. Nurse Owen's eyes were red and swollen. Lovely Nurse Owens, it just proved what a nice person she was.

We caught the service bus back to the hospital, and for the rest of the afternoon we talked of nothing else but our Technicolour experience, and felt also that we had taken the struggles and achievements of that dog to our hearts.

It had been a magical afternoon that for me at least would never to be forgotten.

Chapter 20.

The winter of 1948 set in with a vengeance, and Fortitude Ward felt like an icebox. Upon waking up on a morning I could feel the icy air in my lungs as the clanging enamel bowls heralded our dreaded coughing and spitting routine. When leaning over the edge of our beds in the sub-zero temperature the cruel air nipped at our necks, shoulders and arms, despite our thick long-sleeved nightdresses. How wonderful it was to eventually enter the corridor where the warm air was. Those of us who were desperate for the toilets went to the washroom whilst the remainder crowded in front of the huge coal fire in the dining room for a minute or two, basking in the radiant heat.

No matter what the state of the weather our twice daily walks were hardly ever cancelled. Appropriate foul weather clothing would be issued, so whether there was deep snow, icy rain or even hailstones, we walked. Due to the nights spent exposed to the winter our lips became chapped and our faces were sore. My bottom lip cracked open and would not heal, despite the cream the nurses kept applying. If I forgot and smiled broadly, my lip would again burst and bleed profusely. We all had problems with chilblains on our feet, some even had them on their hands.

Despite Fortitude Ward being so cold, we nevertheless had to lie on our beds for thirty minutes each day following the midday meal. Nurses would wrap us in thick blankets to keep us warm.

At bedtime I hated having to leave the warmth of the dining room and enter Fortitude Ward. Beyond the wire netting everywhere would be white with frost, Our counterpanes felt damp, yet when we climbed into our beds we were surprisingly warm. The nurse would come round the beds ensuring we were all tightly tucked in - so tightly that we could hardly turn over. We would put the top sheet over our faces to try to prevent the icy air entering our lungs.

At night-time the shutters were lowered a quarter distance towards the top of the wall but acquired rows of icicles that were like rods of crystal. The bottom half of the netting therefore remained open to the elements. When there was winter rain and a stiff wind was blowing then the staff had to pull our beds away from the washes of water.

One might assume that the spartan outdoor sleeping in such bitter temperatures would invite pneumonia, but during the winter months of 1948 I cannot recall a girl even catching a cold.

January and February, needless to say, seemed endless. The daily schedule became monotonous. The only high points were visiting days, and although adverse weather made the journey arduous for my parents they never missed visiting me. On one occasion the bus my dad was returning home on got stuck in a blizzard on the Pennine Hills. The driver and the passengers were stranded on the moors until a snowplough arrived to clear the snow away. On my mam's next visit I learned how frantically worried she had been when my dad did not arrive home until the following day.

Slowly but surely though the days began to lengthen. That cruel winter released its grip on the frozen land and the sun began to climb a little higher in the sky. February gave way to March and a prelude to Spring was in the air. The songs of the birds seeking mates once again heralded the dawn with their morning chorus. On the trees buds began to swell and warmer breezes replaced the icy winds. By the middle of March Spring had at last arrived. Our spirits soared, not only because of the rebirth of Nature, but also because the next medicals were to be held during the last week in March.

I had begun to feel confident that my discharge date was near, for I had survived a fierce winter sleeping in the open without as much as a sneeze - surely I was cured, for how else had I staved off the winter colds and flu?

Chapter 21.

Flora and Rebecca were firm friends. Christine and I were close to both Flora and Rebecca, and we four were always together. We blended perfectly. Fora was fun-loving, she never looked on the dark side of life and her zest for living rubbed off on us all. Christine was the thoughtful one. She would weigh up the pros and cons of any situation and make a judgement based on all the information she had to hand, and we all valued her diplomacy. As for Rebecca, it was of paramount importance that her friends liked her., and if she thought she had offended one of us by a thoughtless word or act, then she was unhappy until the problem was sorted. Rebecca had a lovely smile. It was hard to believe she had been that peevish girl whom no one had liked when she had first been admitted. As for for me, I was their friend too. Just what they gained from my friendship I was never able to discover, but it seemed that in spite of my own view of myself I was important to them.

During the long winter months I had managed to stay out of trouble, but all that was to change.

Once again I misplaced my comb.

Just as I had previously done I gazed at an empty hook as I replaced my toothbrush. My comb was not there. Rebecca and Flora and Christine helped me to search for it, but without success, for just as before it had disappeared without trace.

What would Sister Devereaux have to say this time? More importantly, how would she deal with my carelessness? To lose a comb once was bad enough, but to be careless enough to lose another did not bear thinking about. Sister's chastisement of me when she was cross had been a frightening ordeal for me. I stood in awe of her and dreaded falling out of her favour. Even when she was being nice to me her aura of authority and supremacy created an invisible barrier I could not face.

Upon realising I had lost my comb Nurse Stubbs sent me to Sister Devereaux's desk.

Sister looked at me and asked:

"What do you want, Eleanor?"

I explained.

I saw the annoyance in her face as she snapped:

"Go and look for it, right now!"

Then she added:

"And don't you dare return without it!"

To my shame some tears began to well up, which I knew she had seen. What a cry-baby she must have thought I was.

I searched for my comb once again but to no avail. I felt wretched. How could I return to her and tell her I had failed to find it? Yet what was the alternative?

Striving to hold back my tears I approached her desk and in a nervous voice I told her I still could not find my comb.

Once again she loaned me a comb. My stomach was churning and I found it difficult to eat my breakfast.

The walk that morning was to Heather Hill, but as the others fetched their coats Sister summoned me to her desk.

"Eadie," she said sternly. "You are not going anywhere until you have found your comb. There is no morning walk for you. You must remain in the hospital and search for it. Failure to locate it will lead to you having to answer to me for your negligence, and I don't think I need to spell out what the consequences will be should you fail - do I Eadie?"

I replied immediately with a trembling voice.

"I will try to find it, Sister," I said.

I miserably watched as everyone else put on their coats and hats and set off on their walk without a care in the world, whilst I should remain in the hospital with what seemed the impossible task of finding my comb.

Sister Devereaux was at her desk as I wandered, her attention was focussed on a pile of blue folders and she paid no attention to me. Then I left the dining room after I had searched every inch of it and I left for the washroom. Now very alone I could let my tears flow. What was the point of searching once again? I Had already looked twice. Standing in a corner of the washroom I slithered my back down the wall until I was in a crouching position, and I sobbed.

I really felt I could not face Sister Devereaux again with her cold eyes and aloof manner. How I wished I was at home again with my mam and dad.

I cried until I could cry no more. Then I began to think logically. Where had I not looked? The only place I could think of to search again was my locker. So wiping my tears on the sleeve of my jumper I opened the washroom door and saw Sister Devereaux walking towards Courtesy Ward. She stopped to speak with Nurse Whiteley. I stood watching as Sister spoke to Nurse Whiteley in an important manner, walked on a short way and then turned back and spoke to Nurse Whiteley again and even smiled at her.

Perhaps if I could only find my comb my troubles might be over.

I waited until the corridor was clear and then proceeded to Fortitude Ward where I once again searched my locker, but to no avail.

Then just as I was about to despair I thought of moving my locker to see if my comb was underneath and to my absolute joy there it was.

I picked up my comb and kissed it in triumph.

Jubilantly I returned to the dining room but found Sister Devereaux's desk was unattended. I returned to the corridor which was silent except for distant noises from beyond the fire doors.

I was used to constantly being in the company of other children and so to find myself alone was a strange experience.

Unsure of what to do next I wandered along to my left and after some way I stopped in total surprise, for the 'forbidden door' was open.

I looked up the corridor and then looked down the corridor but there was not a soul in sight, not even a cleaner.

I stared at the doorway that had dominated stories of the dark and dreadful.

Should I risk a quick glance?

For what seemed a long time I stood pondering and taking two steps forward and then back. Then when there was still no one near I reached the doorway and I looked inside.

The room was brightly lit and was full of technical equipment, none which was the least bit familiar. On the floor was laid a thick mat and on the mat was laid a boy who looked to be around the same age as me. He was laid face down but with his face turned aside and while a bright lamp like a summer sun shining down on him. He wore goggles, which were dark, and there was no indication that he could see me looking at him.

I stood spellbound, for the boy was naked, and he looked beautiful. The light shining down on him gave his skin an unearthly glow and I found myself suppressing a desire to step into the room and to touch the boy to confirm that he was real.

Then a nurse in the room, but who was out of my line of vision, asked the boy to turn over. Then on hearing her voice a spell was broken and I very quickly withdrew.

It was just an ordinary room after all, though filled with extraordinary things. I thought of all the scary stories I had heard or made up for others and knew none of them would be the same now.

I saw Sister Devereaux walk through the door from Courtesy Ward and on seeing me she immediately spoke.

"Have you found your comb, Eadie?"

"Yes, Sister," I replied and I held it up for her to see.

"Give it to me," she said, her face unsmiling.

I handed her my comb, while I felt a little mystified as to why she should want it.

Why had she not told me to return it to the hook in the washroom?

Then she glanced at me.

"Select a book from the schoolroom to read until the other girls return from their walk," she said.

This I did.

However I could not concentrate for it seemed that for the second time that day I had lost my comb. I decided, that the act of losing the comb in the first place had still broken the rule and that I was not yet out of trouble.

Teatime came, and I was resigned to my fate. I was waiting to hear the clear voice of Sister Devereaux calling me to approach her, and I did not have to wait very long.

"Eadie! Please approach my desk!"

I walked over to her desk.

A feeling of weakness had overtaken me and I no longer feared her chastisement, I was quite willing to accept whatever discipline she had decided upon.

Sister reached into her desk drawer and drew out my comb. It was the very same comb I had surrendered to her that morning.

"Here is your comb, Eadie. Please do not lose it again."

I took the comb from her hand and stood waiting for what was to come next. However as I looked at her face I was surprised to see not anger, but mirth, for there was a twinkle in her eye.

I blinked, for I thought I was imagining things, but no there was no trace of anger in her face at all. In fact she looked like she was trying not to smile.

"Go and sit down, Eleanor," she said.

I could not believe it. Was that it? No punishment?

I returned to my seat feeling grateful but also confused.

I sat watching Sister Devereaux.

She had her elbow on the desk with her hand on her forehead and was looking down at the paper on which she was writing. I noticed that her shoulders were shaking slightly, but her hand hid her face.

Then she lowered her hand, looked up and fixed her eyes on me and then she began openly laughing. She shook with laughter, and I knew her laughter was something to do with me.

What was so funny? Surely it could not be anything to do with losing my comb.

Mystified, I looked down at my comb, but when I read the name-tag I knew exactly why she was amused. For gone was my name and instead a new name tag had been attached with the word '*Forget-Me-Not*' etched on it.

I looked up at her gingerly and slowly I began to smile back at her, at first hesitantly, and then broadly.

I was so surprised that Sister Devereaux had a sense of humour. It was yet another facet of her confounding personality that I was slowly but surely beginning to understand.

From thereon Sister Devereaux, when in an affable mood affectionately called me '*Forget-Me-Not.*"

Now that my worries were over, my thoughts returned to my earlier discovery and I began to recount to my friends what I had seen behind the forbidden door. Then I suggested that we should be the ones to tell the others.

Christine placed a hand on my arm.

"We cannot do that," she said. "Or we shall have no more proper stories at bedtimes."

Christine then glanced at the others.

"It must be our secret."

There was, however, one secret that even Christine did not know. about, The bright lamp and the other equipment was beyond our comprehension, but altogether seemed generally medical. It was my memory of the luminous figure that I did not disclose The memory of the shining boy became mine and mine alone.

Chapter 22.

We awoke one sunlit morning. Spring breezes were softly caressing our faces as we lay in our beds in Fortitude Ward. April had arrived and the land was beginning to stir with new life. Daffodils were swaying in the gardens, along with wild flowers associated with the hopeful season.

All during the winter months Christine and Flora had been telling me about the rock pools and how delightful they were, so when Sister Devereaux announced that the shoreline was to be our destination that morning then Christine and Flora were delighted.

I stepped out into the spring morning air feeling joyful as we made our way beyond the promenade and onto the shore to this as yet undiscovered delight.

We all spread out over the the rock-flats kneeling and exploring. Christine and I crouched down and found tiny marine worlds where all manner of tiny creatures co-existed. The sand margins were wet or else thick with seaweed, while shellfish clung tightly to rocks and try as I might I could not dislodge them. The air was noisy with the cries of gulls while the pure salty air filled our lungs as we scrambled here and there.

I began to collect shells. There were many varieties, including many spiral shells that I particularly liked. Many were smooth little bulbous types that Christine said were winkles and I decided to collect those too. Razorshells, cockleshells, whelks and half-scallops were all brought to my inspection where my friends informed of me of their types and I crammed them into my skirt pockets, along with quite a quantity of sand.

What a wonderful morning I had! The sun was warm on my face and the breeze was so comforting and were the rules of the hospital not still in force we would surely have stayed longer.

Prior to lunch I examined the shells I had collected and then I placed them in lines on the internal window ledge above our bench while our meals were served. I ate ravenously, for the sea air had made me so hungry. After dinner I put my favourite shells back in my pockets and we then lay on our beds for the customary thirty minutes. After this we rose with the intention of going along to the schoolroom, except that Nurse Mollett entered Fortitude Ward and ordered us all back into the dining-room.

The minute we entered the dining room we knew something had annoyed Sister, simply by observing her face, for her blue eyes were cold as she considered us.

She raised her arm and pointed with her forefinger at the windows overlooking Fortitude Ward.

"Who is responsible for this?" she said.

We all looked in the direction she was pointing and saw half a dozen winkles making their way up the panes of glass.

Many of the girls had seen me playing with shells before mealtime so I knew I could not hide in the crowd.

Sister's face remained resolute.

"Well! I am waiting!" said Sister, eyeing us all keenly.

"Please Sister," I began and I flinched when her gaze quickly settled on me. "I think it might have been me."

"Eadie. Please approach my desk," she said before addressing the others girls. "The rest of you proceed to the schoolroom."

I stood before Sister's desk while everyone else trooped out of the room and down the corridor, leaving me alone with Sister Devereaux.

She came from behind her desk.

"Empty your pockets," she said sternly.

I hesitated.

"Immediately," she added.

I began to fumble in my pockets, lifting out the shells, together with sprinkles of sand and placed the shells on the blotting pad on her desk.

Then she picked up some of the shells and examined them carefully, and then looked at me with those eyes that I could now read so well and that were sharp with disapproval.

Out of panic spoke first.

"Please Sister, I did not know they were alive, " I said, my voice shaking. "I thought they were pretty and I just wanted them to play with."

"You did not know they were alive?" she asked incredulously. "How old are you Eadie?"

I swallowed as my throat constricted.

"I am ten, Sister," I said.

She walked over to the windows of the dining-room that gave a view down into Fortitude Ward, and saw the winkles had turned about at the top and were now slowly descending.

After studying their movements she addressed me.

"You are to go the schoolroom and ask Miss Moran to give you a book on marine life and then you are to bring that book to me," she said.

"Yes Sister," I replied.

I practically ran through Courtesy Ward and into the school room where I asked Miss Moran for the requested book. Then I returned just as quickly to the dining room where I handed the book to Sister.

Then with uncertainty no doubt evident on my face I watched Sister Devereaux perusing the pages of the book.

"Here is an article about the winkle," she said," she said. "I want you to memorise this and be word perfect by teatime tomorrow. Do I make myself clear?"

"Yes, Sister," I replied meekly.

Sister sat straighter in the chair behind her desk.

"If you complete this task then that will be the end of the matter, for it did not escape my notice that you owned up to being responsible."

Then she returned to such papers that she was concerned with.

"That is all, Eadie. You may now go to school," she said.

I left the dining room with the marine life book in my hand and I felt as if a heavy weight had been lifted from me.

I decided that I would complete the task had set for me to a standard approaching perfection. I rose to the challenge of learning the description of winkles bit by bit.

After teatime it was my unusual duty to educate the other girls by reciting the text exactly while Sister, having the said book before her, saw that the penance was done. It is the most curious thing to deliver such concise knowledge in so purposeful a way to an audience who had absolutely no interest in it.

Then strangely, my enforced lesson on winkles whetted my appetite for learning more about the inhabitants of rock pools. During the days that followed I read what I could of the watery oases that give shelter to such unexpected companions between the tides.

On my subsequent trips to the rock pools I was able to identify the clinging shells as barnacles, which live firmly clamped to the rocks in vast numbers. I knew also the Spiny Starfish and several of the darting little fish that moved rapidly about. There was also the Beadlet Anemone that became a small blob of jelly when it contracted its tentacles as my fingers touched it. Then there the Limpets, that semed the elder brothers of the barnacles and were just as immovable. Then the Coral Weed, having pink tufts of lime-armoured branches that remained just below the water's surface.

I could identify all of the seashells, the daintiest of which were some spiral shells that now had a name. They were called Needle Shells.

Learning about the common winkle had opened up an appreciation of rock pools that made me a modest expert on those days that our walks went that way. The sharp aroma that braced me when I was walking the strands was no longer a mystery, it was iodine, released by the seaweeds when parts of them were decaying. They were worlds in miniature that had had opened up to me, and for the rest of my time at the hospital I was eager to learn some more about the little depths and about the awkwardly acquainted creatures that could be found in them.

Chapter 23.

Medicals had been carried out the previous month, and it was disappointment once again that neither Christine, Flora and rebecca or myself were discharged. Neither was Dorothy, who had now sunk into a darker depression. She was removed herself from our influence and not even Sister Devereaux could talk her round to accepting the doctor's decision.

We were all wondering what would become of Dorothy.

We did not have to wait long to find out, and what's more what happened a few weeks later might well have come from the pen of Enid Blyton rather the hum-drum routine of Fortitude Ward.

It began with the wire netting.

In the lower corner of the netting next to Fortitude Ward, the elements plus general wear and tear had caused the wire netting to break away from where it was attached to the low wall. The result was a small hole. One of the girls decided to use it as the subject of a bedtime story. She thrilled us all with a tale of a masked intruders dressed in black entering that way in the dead of night. The silver blade of a dagger was described as glinting in his hand as he made his way to The Forbidden Door. There a rendezvous with a demon doctor resulted in the plotting of evil deeds, in much the same way as every other demon doctor plotted them.

Our pulses were racing as we listened spellbound, and afterwards the storyteller was applauded. The ward gradually became silent.

Then Dorothy spoke out in clear tones.

"If an intruder could get in," she said with fascination, "then maybe someone could also get out."

Soon after the door opened and the nurse turned out the lights, after which there was no talking.

I lay thinking about what Dorothy had said, and wondering if she would try to climb out through the hole in the middle of the night.

The first thing everyone did upon waking the next morning was to look in the direction of Dorothy's bed, and we were all relieved to see that she had not wriggled through the hole in the middle of the night.

During our morning walk there were ripples of conversation in hushed tones going up and down the 'crocodile' and the gist of the whispers was the speculation that Dorothy was indeed intending to climb out through the hole in the meshing one night and go home.

We were all filled with a sense of adventure, fuelled by the numerous adventure stories we had read, so that we were only too willing to help her. make her plan as a something to do. The nurses were unaware of these conversations going back and forth, with the result that during our talking time that evening we solemnly promised Dorothy that we would help her in any way we could and referred to her plan as '*Moonlight.*'

It became an exciting game. The fact that Dorothy would have no money for transport did not count, for none of us took the plan seriously. Everyone agreed that Moonlight had become both the best bedtime story and the best day-time intrigue we had ever conjured together.

During the following weeks there were secretive talks in hushed tones on how the Moonlight plan could be realised. Meanwhile Dorothy, who normally refused our friendship, found herself at the centre of attention. She was the storyteller of all storytellers when talking time came and also the inventor of this extraordinary secret game that we could play during daylight hours.

There were many means suggested of how Dorothy could make her getaway. Most were considered impractical and were dismissed.

After two days we were left with two options.

During the nightly hymn singing in the dining room the nurses stood with their backs to us, thereby obscuring Sister Devereaux's view if she should she walk over to the window to inspect us. The night staff did not come on duty until the singing was over, which allowed for for a brief period when Fortitude Ward was not under supervision. However, this would mean Dorothy would not be able to enter the dining room to retrieve her day clothes, and there was no way to smuggle them into Fortitude Ward at bedtime, given the scrutiny of the nurses and Sister Devereaux herself.. At the time of the hymn singing it would also be daylight, since it was April, and so it was decided that Dorothy should wait until the night staff came on duty and then wait for a suitable moment.

Sister Kilshaw, when not on the move would be seated at her desk in Patience Ward. Meanwhile the night nurse would be constantly patrolling and checking on all three wards. We had noticed however that on occasions neither Sister Kilshaw nor the night nurse were present, which would be an ideal opportunity for Dorothy to sneak down the corridor and fetch her clothes. Then after that, and lying fully dressed in her bed, she would wait for the next unsupervised moment to make her escape.

There were, however, two more things to avoid.

First, the lamplighter.

Every evening the lamplighter's appearance would coincide with the first cover of darkness. He would walk by with a long pole, lighting the gaslights in the street. The following morning, as was his duty, he returned to switch the gaslights off again. Dorothy would have to wait until the lamplighter had passed by and turned on all the gaslights within sight of the hospital and wait until he had walked on.

Such was the precision of the planning that we could think of no better one. It was as if the game called Moonlight had reached its endpoint.

However our interest in Dorothy and in Moonlight, although fiercely exciting, was eclipsed the very next day, because of a frog.

Chapter 24.

The following morning Sister decided that our morning walk would be to the park, with nurses Owens and Mollett accompanying us, so that we put on our coats and hats and stepped out into the spring sunshine. The birds were singing, insects were buzzing, and we walked out glad to be alive on such a lovely day.

Upon arriving at the park we ran about the lawns and gardens, played on the swings and roundabouts, and then Christine and I wandered off together and sat down on a park bench, whilst Rebecca and Flora were off in the near distance swinging away happily.

Christine happened to noticed a pamphlet on the ground, which someone had thrown away, and picking it up she began to contemplate it.

"Eleanor, do you know how to make an aeroplane from paper?"

"No I don't," I said.

Therefore Christine began folding the pamphlet while I became totally absorbed in watching her do it.

Flora joined us, but I was so engrossed in watching Christine that I paid little attention to what Flora said and neither did Christine.

Christine was sat folding in earnest and had her tongue stuck out of the side of her mouth as she proceed with deep concentration.

Flora continued to talk to us, gesticulating with her arms.

When we finally looked at Flora she snapped at us for ignoring her.

"I have something very important to show you!" Flora said in her usual dramatic way, but when we appeared to be again engrossed in making the paper plane she paced about.

"Then you will never ever know what it is," she said and she strode off angrily.

"Please come back!" Christine called out but Flora was walking haughtily back to the playground, presumably to find Rebecca.

"We should leave her alone," said Christine, "because she can get so huffy at times."

When Flora did come around she was still out of patience and so we made it worth her while by explaining the paper plane and how it would make its maiden flight.

We had the plane glide here and there for a while, but it was not altogether a success, so that Flora went elsewhere.

Rebecca came over to ask us where Flora was and we were just about to say we thought Flora was with her, when our conversation was interrupted a scream of absolute terror.

We three stared across the park and saw Nurse Owens in some terrible distress.

Our paper plane was forgotten and we ran across the grass as fast as we could to see what was going on. When we got there a crowd of children and some park bystanders had gathered to see what was the matter.

Flora had been down at the lake, had picked up a frog and decided to put it in Nurse Owens' coat pocket.

Then feeling movement and investigating Nurse Owens had demonstrated most vividly to everyone that she was terrified of frogs.

Nurse Mollett was apologising to the strangers whilst also calling the girls to order, though everyone was laughing at Nurse Owens' reaction.

Nurse Mollett was furious.

"You causing such a fright to Nurse Owens will be reported to Sister Devereaux just as soon as we return to the hospital," she said angrily.

Flora stood scowling.

"But it was only a joke," then she made another performance of flinging her arms about.

"How was I to know she was going to scream like that?"

When Sister Devereaux heard of the incident she was beside herself with fury and Flora was reprimanded in front of all of us.

"Wilson!" she said. "You will go to bed at six o' clock each evening until further notice!"

I had never seen Sister so cross before, and her temper seemed to burn across the rest of us so that we were all as quiet as mice and hardly daring to breathe.

Then Sister addressed us all.

"What happened in the park today was unforgivable. Each and every one of you has made a public spectacle of yourselves. You have brought shame not only upon yourselves but upon the hospital."

Then she banged her fist loudly down upon her desk.

"I am thoroughly ashamed of you all!"

She looked sternly around the room and at every girl in turn, then said:

"You will all go to bed at six o'clock, with no talking until I have reviewed my decision."

Not one girl spoke.

Privately I felt the punishment was unjust, because after all Christine and Rebecca and I had been quite removed from the disturbance when it had begun. We had not laughed or made a scene, yet one look at Sister's face told us we had absolutely no chance of reasoning with her.

Then with growing clarity I understood that if we had listened to Flora at the outset she would not have become so attention-seeking in the first place. She would not have gone down to the lake and she would not have happened upon the frog.

Nevertheless we began our penance.

How miserable it was to have to go to bed at six o' clock with no talking time. Flora had finally gone over the top with her mischief, and she certainly knew we all felt resentful, but she kept a stiff upper lip and weathered the storm.

The next morning Sister had not calmed down, and we were all very careful not to get on the wrong side of her. Even the slightest misdemeanour could have had severe consequences.

What really worried us though, was that there had been no sign of Nurse Owens after the frog incident. We all liked her and missed her, so we aksed Nurse Mollett where she was.

"Nurse Owens has gone away on holiday," was her reply.

We did not of course believe her because we all felt certain that her sudden absence had something to do with the frog. We went to bed on the second of our early nights wishing we knew what had happened to Nurse Owens.

The next day we received some information from the outpost of shoe cleaners. They alleged to have heard two nurses talking about Nurse Owens, saying what a shame it was that she was to be dismissed from her job for making a public spectacle of herself in front of the children.

This news upset everyone, for we all liked Nurse Owens. Flora found it all too much and burst into tears.

"I never the joke would go so badly,"Flora wailed.

Then she faced us in the most tragic way.

"I cannot carry on like this. I have to find some way to put things right - but what can I do?"

Christine replied.

"Nothing can be done," she said, "because we cannot undo what has already been done."

Flora refused to believe this and after some thought she explained her plan.

"I am going to approach Sister Devereaux and beg her to reinstate Nurse Owens."

Flora stood where she had our complete attentions.

"I am going to rehearse what I am going to say," she said finally with a tone of expertise.

None of us could imagine having the nerve to approach Sister in her present mood, for she might not be prepared to listen to Flora,and might even punish her more. Her plan caused a more general unease. We were all fearful that Flora might make things worse for everyone.

The next morning after breakfast Flora raised her hand and asked Sister if she could approach her desk.

Sister looked coldly at her, and then gave her permission.

At that moment I could not believe that Flora would even stood up, for the look on Sister's face would have definitely put me off.

However, incredibly. I was wrong because Flora did stand up and she did approach Sister's desk.

"Well, Wilson. What is it that you want to say?" Sister asked.

Flora cleared her throat and began her well-rehearsed speech.

"Please, Sister. I am truly sorry for putting a frog in Nurse Owens' pocket. It was a horrid thing that I did, and I deserve my punishment."

She paused nervously and then continued.

"Nurse Owrns did not do anything wrong, Sister. It was me - just me - and she does not deserve to be dismissed. So please take her back, because we all love her and we need her."

Flora took a faltering step backwards whilst ending her speech.

"That is all I wanted to say, Sister."

Fora then stood with her head bowed, waiting for Sister to speak.

"Sit down, Wilson," Sister said.

Flora returned to her seat and I believe as she did so that she had the admiration of every girl in the room. She had dared to approach Sister, rehearsed what she would say and she had said it well.

Sister looked around the room, her face pinched with anger.

"Hands on heads. Everyone this minute!" she ordered, pronouncing every syllable.

There was a fearful intake of breath as we each girl put our hands on her head.

136

I wondered what was coming next.

For five minutes we sat there, whilst Sister remained seated at her desk attending to her paperwork, though her face suggested she was deeper in thought.

She then looked up:

"You may all now be at ease."

We lowered our arms and sat waiting to see what would happen next.

"Come here, Wilson," she said, and Flora immediately jumped up and walked briskly over to Sister's desk.

"Why do you think I dismissed Nurse Owens?"

Flora replied slowly.

"Because of the trouble over the frog, Sister."

"You are not paying attention, Wilson. I will rephrase me question. Why do you assume Nurse Owens has been dismissed?"

Flora was floundering a little.

"Because," she hesitated, "because we have not seen her since the frog scared her," is all Flora could say.

"Return to your seat, Wilson," was Sister's reply.

Sister's gaze travelled across us.

"You will continue to retire at six o' clock. Your walk today will be to the promenade."

Sister made her usual inspection of our coats and shoes, after which we set off on our morning walk with heavy hearts.

We returned and following school we took our places as usual in the dining room for our midday meal. We could hear the trolley approaching in the corridor. Sister marched across to the dining-room door and opened it and she spoke to the dinner lady, who waited with her trolley just outside the door.

Then Sister walked back to her desk and sat down.

"Flora Wilson, please stand up."

Flora stood up nervously.

"I accept your apology of this morning, and you can resume your seven o' clock bedtime. Please sit down."

Flora gratefully sat down.

Then Sister addressed us all.

"As for the rest of you, your six o' clock bedtime punishment is at an end."

"*Thank you, Sister,*" we all chanted.

"Finally," Sister said, "I would like to make clear to you that Nurse Owens is still in the employ of this establishment and will be returning to work on Monday. That is all. Enjoy your meals"

She then walked to the door and allowed the dinner lady to enter.

The incident of the frog was over.

The frog was not mentioned again and Sister Devereaux reverted to her usual self.

Nurse Owens, as predicted by Sister, returned to work on the following Monday. When we asked where she had been she seemed surprised to be asked.

""I have been visiting my grandparents in Wales, I have," she said without hesitation.

We still had our suspicions. We thought it strange that Nurse Owens went on holiday immediately after her encounter with the frog, and wondered if Sister had indeed suspended her.

Flora, who was still feeling insecure, apologised profusely to Nurse Owens, who in her turn took Flora in her arms.

"You are forgiven, Flora" said Nurse Owens warmly, "provided you never, and I mean never, do anything like that again."

Flora, and indeed all of us, resolved that Nurse Owens and any available frog should not meet any time soon.

Such was our devotion to our pretty Welsh nurse.

Chapter 25.

A few weeks went by uneventfully, until our thoughts returned to Dorothy, and her exciting game of 'Moonlight.' It soon became the subject of storytelling at bedtime, with tales of girls climbing through the netting and disappearing and having exciting adventures. What none of us realised was that for Dorothy it was not make-believe at all, it was serious, though as I say, with our being fully involved in the game, none of us appreciated this.

Dorothy could remember every detail of the plans we had drawn up a few weeks earlier. As far as we were concerned Dorothy was simply taking the game to whole new levels of excitement.

Then one one night when the hymn singing was over and the day nurses went off duty a moment came when all was quiet. Then quite suddenly Dorothy got out of bed and put on her slippers.

"I am going to fetch my clothes from the dining room" she whispered.

I could hardly believe my eyes as Dorothy walked to the door, up the two steps, and then, after opening the door carefully, she sneaked forward and waited. After a few glances to make sure all was clear, she went through into the corridor and quietly closed the door behind her. Then as we watched through the corridor windows we saw the top of her blonde head bobbing up and down as she sprang along to towards the dining room. Then after a pause, which was surely like an eternity for us, the bobbing blonde hair came back along the corridor and back into Fortitude Ward.

She was empty handed.

None of us had realised that the dining room door was locked at night time, and so Dorothy climbed back into bed. Her plan had not worked, but it did not matter, after all it was only a game.

The next day Dorothy was centre stage and basking in the limelight whilst our eager minds were focussed on thinking up an even better plan. We wanted the game called Moonlight to go on forever.

The next night when the silvery moon made its lonely watch of all that was nocturnal, a little ghost-like figure had surely flitted across the lawns of the hospital and tugging in vain at the chains of the gates. For being all fast asleep we could no longer know what plan, if any, was being executed. Somewhere around the perimeter there must have been a means to climb a wall, while one bed in Fortitude Ward was empty, with a pillow stuffed down between the sheets to make it appear Dorothy was there.

Dorothy had climbed through the hole in the netting in the middle of the night wearing only her nightgown and slippers.

The following morning it was quickly discovered that Dorothy was missing. True to our pledge none of us admitted to knowing anything at all about it, but the suspicion in the nurses' faces weighed heavily on us. The hole in the netting was noticed and was immediately repaired.

Faced with the fact that Moonlight had been real we were all anxiously wondering whether Dorothy had actually managed to find her way home, It was more likely however that she was wandering around lost and miserable.

We did not have long to wait, for later that day we saw Matron talking to two policemen with Dorothy standing beside them. Then our nurses called us to step away so that we were not able to watch for longer.

Later on we had to endure a long speech delivered by Matron to us all on the subject of absconding, and leaving us in no doubt how dangerous it was. There then followed an equally long speech from Sister Devereaux, who wanted to know if another girl knew what Dorothy had been planning to do. We all remained faithful to our secrecy and denied all knowledge whatsoever.

On our next visiting day every mother and father gave their child a lecture, warning them against doing anything so foolish. A news item on the radio had reported that a child had gone missing from a hospital on the Wirral and subsequent announcements described the success of the police after their exhaustive attempts to find her.

We never saw Dorothy again.

Chapter 26.

It was the month of May and the weather was glorious. The sun was shining high in the sky and the whole of our little world seemed radiant and beautiful. The windows of the dining-room were thrown open, as were the French windows of Patience Ward, letting in the pure air that was fragrant with blossom.

Sleeping on Fortitude Ward was no longer a hardship, it was now a pleasure. We were going to bed in daylight and we were able to watch the sunset in the west and watch the moon above trees that were freshly dressed in their gowns of tender leaves.

The half-hour rest period after our midday meals was also pleasant as we lay on our beds whilst soft breezes spun about us.

Although I wanted desperately to go home, and waited anxiously after every medical check, I was not unhappy in the hospital. I was become accustomed to Sister Devereaux's funny ways. I was well aware that she was far from perfect, for at times she could be extremely caustic when she spoke to nurses, often in front of us (which was doubly humiliating for them.) Then of course there were times when some small matter would cause her temper to rise, or else other times when her discipline seemed to completely overtake her. Nevertheless I was beginning to understand her and make allowances for her shortcomings, for she had many redeeming qualities. Despite her strictness with us all she could be very caring if she thought a girl was genuinely upset. However, unlike the nurses, she never hugged or kissed a girl. Physical content other than holding a girl's hand was totally absent.

Life for me then was very agreeable. I had three sincere friends and had no pressing matters save for hoping that my next medical would result in my discharge.

It was. As it turned out, it was tempting fate to regard oneself oneself free of troubles, as I was soon to find out.

One morning I awoke to the birds' chorus before the night nurse began loudly clanging the enamel bowls.

Christine had not stirred, so I called out her name, but there was still no response. Again I called, this time more loudly and asking her to wake up, but still she did not respond.

The nurse shook her, and Christine sleepily opened her eyes and then spoke.

"I do not feel like coughing today," she whispered.

"It is important that you clear your chest," the night nurse said.

Then Christine snuggled back under the covers and refused to cough.

"I do not feel very well," she said.

The nurse fetched Sister Kilshaw who put a hand to Christine's forehead, then placed a thermometer in Christine's armpit. After checking the reading Sister Kilshaw deliberated before addressing the night nurse.

"She has a slight - t-temperature," she stammered, "and she is to be excused from coughing today."

Christine thankfully pulled the bedclothes around her herself and did not speak, even to me.

When it was time to get up Sister Kilshaw told Christine to stay where she was, but Christine replied.

"I am feeling much better now," she said, "so I shall get up."

As we were washing ourselves and cleaning our teeth, Christine placed her hands on the washbasin and leaned forward, her head bowed.

"Are you alright?" I asked her.

"I will be in a minute," she said, "I felt suddenly very strange.

I felt a sudden unease and I turned towards the door.

"I will fetch the nurse," I said.

Suddenly Christine stood up straight.

"You must not do that," she said. "There are medicals next month and if Sister finds out I am not feeling well then it will be written in her report and that will stand against me being discharged," she said.

Then she looked at me appealingly.

"Please, Eleanor, do as I ask. Do not say anything. Promise.

"I promise," I said reluctantly.

Yet I noticed that tiny beads of sweat were forming on her forehead.

What could I do?

Whilst we were queueing outside the dining room, Sister Devereaux came walking along the corridor. She must have been talking to Sister Kilshaw, for she stopped by Christine, gently took her hand and then led her back down the corridor and into Patience Ward.

A feeling of relief flowed through me on knowing Christine was going to receive extra medical treatment.

It felt odd queuing for medication without Christine by my side, and when breakfast was served I picked up my spoon and began eating my porridge with less enthusiasm than normal, for my mind was on Christine and wondering if she was alright.

Both Rebecca and Flora were most attentive.

"The important thing is that Sister knows," said Flora. "That means everything is going to be alright."alright.

Flora continued.

"Christine will be back with us soon," she said.

Rebecca agreed.

"Whatever she has caught it won't amount to anything," Rebecca said, "after all we are in a hospital."

I wanted to believe Flora and Rebeca, I really did. But they hadn't seen Christine first thing that morning when I could not wake her.

I felt agitated and I pushed my bowl of half-eaten porridge away, for a feeling of nausea had engulfed me.

Sister Devereaux made her usual inspection of us, and decided, as it was a lovely sunny day that we could go and play on Willows Hill.

I normally loved going to Willows Hill because there were lots of rocks, trees and open grassland there where we could run and play. There were also some Roman ruins, and old tombstones with Latin inscriptions, whilst right at the top of the hill there were seats for people to sit and enjoy the view. It was also one of Christine's favourite walks, and the fact that she was not coming with us dampened my enthusiasm.

Today my walking partner would be Flora, and Rebecca would have a different partner. When the crocodile compliment added up to an odd number then the little one at the back walked holding the nurse's hand.

During the walk I resolved to try to remember everything I saw, said and did, because I wanted to relay to Christine mental picture of the beautiful morning, and felt sure that if I described it well enough that she would enjoy listening to it.

After lunch Sister Devereaux called me over to her desk.

"Come here, Eleanor," she said gently, beckoning me to her side.

She held my hand.

"Christine is in Patience Ward. As you already know, she is not feeling very well today. She has been asking to see you, so I want you to sit with Christine instead of lying down in your bed in Fortitude Ward. Come with me."

She led me down the corridor to Patience Ward. Christine was in the bed nearest the French windows next to the fireplace.

I sat beside her, noticing her flushed cheeks and her eyes bright with fever, and when I took her hand in mine her hand felt hot and sticky.

Christine smiled.

"I am so pleased to see you," she said.

I then paused whilst considering my report on the day.

"Would you like to know about our walk to Willows Hill?"

She nodded and smiled.

I told her about the beautiful day and the trees with their fresh green leaves and their twigs laden with blossom, so heavy that some of the branches were weighed towards the ground. The branches of the smaller trees had been gently swaying in the summer breeze and had looked like white waterfalls of blossom while the grasses beneath were strewn with fallen petals. All of the May wild flowers were raising their little heads to the sun, whilst the bees were busy climbing inside them. There had been so many birds with younger ones following them around with open beaks -.

I stopped talking, for I noticed that Christine was no longer listening, for she was sound asleep.

I continued to sit holding her hand until Sister Devereaux returned and gently released our hands and led me to the schoolroom for my lesson.

I found it difficult to get through the rest of that day and could not assume any interest in either school or the afternoon walk. It was not the same without Christine beside me and I kept seeing her in my mind's eye laid in bed looking so poorly.

After teatime Sister Devereaux called me over.

"Eleanor, would you like to sleep in Patience Ward with Christine tonight?"

I did not even need to think before giving my answer.

"Oh! Yes please, Sister!" I said, "I would like that."

Then Sister studied me.

"Do you want to enjoy your playtime, or would you like to go to bed now?"

It was only six o' clock but once again my answer was immediate.

"I want to go to bed now, please, and be with Christine."

She led me along to Patience Ward.

"I think the bed on the other side of the fireplace is a little to far. Would you like to sleep opposite Christine?" she asked.

I said that I would.

Christine was so happy to see me, just as I was so pleased to see her.

Sister helped me to undress and I was soon tucked up in bed.

There was only Christine and I in the ward, for the other patients were in the dining room enjoying their play hour, so we had the ward all to ourselves.

We chatted about all sorts of things, though always those subjects that I knew would interest her. I reminded her of times when we had laughed so loud together, such as when we went to see the Lassie film and Nurse Owens had cried. After much talking we laid in our beds smiling at each other. She was very soon too tired to speak and not answering me very often and occasionally motioning with her hand that she agreed with me.

We lapsed into a comfortable silence and then she spoke.

"How very kind it was of Sister to allow us some time together like this," she said.

Then after another silence she said.

"I am sorry, but I am feeling very tired, " she said. "Goodnight Eleanor."

She closed her eyes and I closed mine.

Chapter 27.

Something awoke me; I was not sure what I had heard. At first I could not think where I was, and then I remembered - that I was in Patience Ward.

It was dark. The only light entering was from the dimmed corridor lights that were shining faintly through the windows that overlooked Fortitude Ward.

It must have been the click of the door closing that had awakened me. Then a shadowy figure was standing there. I shut my eyes and peeped through my eyelashes as the figure that was silhouetted against the faint corridor's gleam, silently walked towards Christine's bed. I could make out that it was a woman, but not a nurse, for she was wearing plain clothes. Very quietly she pulled the bed screens around Christine's bed and thus being concealed I could now open my eyes wider. The woman had brought a lamp, for I could now see her silhouette clear and black as she sat on the bed leaning over. She did not speak.

What was this lady she doing here in the middle of the night, and who was she? Did the nursing staff know that she was here? So many thoughts were racing through my mind, yet despite them I did nothing. I simply laid there staring at the illuminated screen.

The other five patients in the ward were sound asleep.

Next I heard a rustle of movement and the lamp was switched off. Carefully the figure pulled back the screen and I quickly narrowed my eyes again.

The figure began to walk towards the door, and then stopped, turned and walked in the direction of my bed so that I shut my eyes tight. Could she be a ghost? Then I knew she was not a ghost because I felt a cool hand press over mine and also I smelled a perfume that was like fine soap. Then I felt soft silky hair brush across my face as I was kissed softly on the forehead. Then after this I saw her walk towards the door. As she made her exit the glow from the corridor lit her face and I saw with amazement that it was

Sister Devereaux. Yet how could it be? Sister Devereaux had gone off duty hours before and was surely asleep at home at so late an hour. Yet the woman had so strongly resembled her! I decided it must have been a trick of the light. It could not have been Sister, for Sister never kissed any of the girls. I simply could not figure it out at all. Another thing puzzled me was that in addition to Christine and myself, five other patients lay sleeping. Why had she not kissed them?

That night I had strange dreams as if I was trying to flee a hidden menace. I needed to escape and was desperately calling for my mother. Dark figures were moving about me.

I awoke to find my bedclothes in a tangle and my pillow on the floor. It was now daybreak and I sat up in bed with the intention of telling Christine about it, but I was stunned when I saw an empty bed with a bare mattress. All the blankets had been removed, even the pillow had gone.

I stared again in disbelief. Where was Christine? Where had they taken her?

Sister Kilshaw walked into the ward, and seeing I was awake she came to my side.

"Christine was taken away in the night," she said.

"Who took her away?" I asked.

She removed her hand from mine as I continued my inquiry.

"When is she coming back?"

"I am n-not sure," Sister Kilshaw said.

She looked towards the door of Patience Ward and took a step in that direction and stopped.

"There is no n-need for you to cough this morning," she said. Then she returned to my bed whilst removing the spectacles from her nose.

"God Bless," she said, then replaced her spectacles and then hurried off and made a swift exit out of Patience Ward and into the corridor.

When I arose, and instead of going straight to the washroom, I entered Fortitude Ward. The bed in which Christine had slept was also stripped down to its mattress. I looked in Christine's locker and saw all of her possessions had been removed.

Then I joined the queue for the washroom.

I had never queued without Christine beside me. Tears began to run down my cheeks.

When I came out of the washroom Sister Devereaux ushered me into the dining room. She led me to one of the benches and then to my surprise she also sat down on the bench opposite. She then held my hand in hers.

"Poor little Forget-Me-Not," she said.

Memories of the silhouetted lady came flooding back but Sister wore different clothes and there was not the fragrant soap about her. All I could smell about Sister Devereaux was the smell of carbolic.

With the absence of Christine my tears began to flow again.

Sister waited until my tears stopped.

"Talk to me Eleanor. I am your friend, you know that, and I want to help you in any way I can."

"Where is Christine?" I asked.

"She was taken away in the night."

I remembered the lady again.

"Did her mummy come for her? I asked her.

"Here mummy and daddy were here last night," she said.

I stared about me.

"Why did Christine not say goodbye? Why did someone not wake me up?"

Then without giving Sister a chance to reply I continued.

"And what about Daisy? Christine promised me," I said angrily.

Sister looked puzzled.

"Who is Daisy?"

"Her dolly. She promised me that before she went home she would give me Daisy, I said."

I wiped at my eyes.

"She promised me, Sister. She promised!"

Sister waited for my full attention.

150

"Listen to me, Eleanor, and listen well. Christine valued your friendship very highly indeed. She was poorly when she left us and therefore she can be forgiven for forgetting about Daisy. Be happy that she has at last found the peace and contentment she was so desperately seeking, just as you will find it one day when you are discharged."

Then Sister sat back.

"At the moment I am fully aware that everything looks grey, for colour has deserted your little world. But the colour has not gone away. To bring the colour back you have to remember Christine with happiness, not sadness. She possessed many fine qualities, some of which she has passed onto you, These will enrich your life. We are all better for having known her."

She held my hand.

"Have you got a smile for me Forget-Me-Not?"

I tried to smile and she smiled back.

"I am always ready to listen any time you feel like talking, Eleanor," she said.

Then she rose."

She walked to the door and gave permission for the queue of children to enter.

Flora and Rebecca came and Flora seemed full of news of some matter that had completely passed me by.

"I have just overheard the nurses saying," Flora gasped, "that flogging in police stations is going to be abolished."

Then Flora flung her arms about.

"And Staff Nurse Briggs says crime is just going to get worse and worse!"

I took this news with no real interest, except to know that the news that Christine had gone home had not yet reached her ears. She would would no doubt find out and be sad, but someone going home was not considered a sad thing. Life in the hospital was going to continue as normal even though Christine had gone home.

Then Rebecca wanted to know what flogging was and was it about making people bleed?

A nurse who had been standing near us all the while explained flogging with some reluctance.

"It is a bunch of twigs - often Birch twigs tied together," she said, "and people who do bad things are whipped with it," she said, and then she whispered, "on their bottoms."

Flora and Rebecca smirked and so did I, but I was wishing that Christine could have been smirking with us, though she was not one to smirk.

Christine was lucky, I decided. She was back home with and her mummy and daddy now. Was she thinking about me? Was she also upset that they had not allowed us to say goodbye? Now she was at home she would be happy. And perhaps, as Sister had said, I should be happy too. It was not going to be easy, being separated from my first real friend and I could not stop thinking about her.

Nothing was going to be the same any more.

After breakfast Sister addressed us.

"Christine is no longer a patient in the hospital, and although she had been unable to to say goodbye to all the friends she had made during her stay, we shall all remember her with warmth and treasure her memory," she said.

I had heard Sister make this announcement many times before, and it had made me wish me wish that my parents would simply turn up and fetch me too, so that I would have no further contact with the hospital. They were announcements that gave me hope, yet on this occasion the words seemed to pierced me.

For a moment there was silence and then there began the soft talking spreading as it always did. Yet for all the respectful things that were said near and far, Christine had been a well-respected member of our little group, but no one would miss her more than I.

Chapter 28.

There seemed, to my young mind, no resolution to the events of that week. I was ship-wrecked with no sign of rescue. However what youth lacks in experience and understanding is made up for by a kind of resilience that makes its appearance in the darkest times, when a child has known so few of them. I had a responsibility to my two friends and even more of a reason, as I saw it, to find my way home just as Christine had done.

A couple of days later when we entered the dining room in the late afternoon for our teatime we saw beside Sister Devereaux's desk an auburn haired girl. Her hair had been cut short and she was seated with her head bowed. Her hands were clenched firmly in her lap.

Sister introduced her.

"You attention please, girls. This is Joyce Woodhead, a new patient in Fortitude Ward. I know you will all make her welcome."

"*Hello, Joyce,*" we all chanted.

A nurse then took Joyce by the hand and led her away.

It seemed I would not be sleeping next to an empty bed that night.

After tea I glanced through the window into Fortitude Ward and saw that Joyce was now in bed.

Poor Joyce, how wretched she must have been feeling. Memories of my first day came flooding back, and of course my memory of how Christine had offered me support and friendship. Now it was time, I decided, for me to do for Joyce what Christine had done for me.

The topic of conversation during playtime between Flora and Rebecca and myself, when we not talking about Christine going home, was Joyce.

Flora had much to say to Rebecca.

"What a stuck-up little snob - *you* were," teased Flora.

Rebecca stuck her tongue out.

"I doubt you were an angel yourself," she teased back.

153

Flora grinned.

"That," she said importantly, "is something you will never know."

Bedtime came.

I entered Fortitude Ward and saw Joyce lying in bed, apparently asleep. I noticed her slippers by her bed and I picked them up and placed them in her locker, recalling the warning that Christine had given me about the creepy crawlies.

Then very gently I spoke to Joyce.

"Are you awake?" I asked.

There was no reply, nor even the slightest movement, so I climbed into bed.

As usual the girls asked if anyone had a story to tell us and there followed a brief babble of chatter that was thrown into relief when one of the older girls said:

"I do not know a story," she said, "but I know a song off by heart.

"Sing it," came many replies.

The singer began.

> *There is a new moon always shining*
> *Down a pathway meant for two,*
> *There is a shadow too reclining*
> *Down Sweetheart Avenue.*
> *There is a path that leads to Loveland,*
> *And folks they say it's true.*
> *There is a for those who go there*
> *Down Sweetheart Avenue.*
> *It is just around the corner*
> *No matter where you are,*
> *And you will always find it*
> *Beneath your lucky star.*
> *When the boy you meet at seven*
> *Whispers 'Darling, I love you.'*
> *You will be on your way to Heaven*
> *Down Sweetheart Avenue.*

We all begged her to sing it once again, and by the end of the thirty minutes' talking time we all knew the tune and were well on our way to remembering the lyrics too. Throughout the various attempts to sing together Joyce lay silent. Surely she could not have slept through the din we made.

The lights were then switched off and we listened to the day shift nurses singing hymns, and we watched all of the pretty nurses going off duty and mingling with the boys at the gate. That song suddenly seemed so fitting in view of the many romantic little scenes at the gates of the hospital.

The following morning I tried again to talk to Joyce, but she was not interested in talking either to me or to anyone. Her eyes were swollen from crying, and she refused to cough into the bowl, despite the efforts of the nurse and Sister Kilshaw.

I persevered whether she listened to me or not.

I gave her the instructions that had been given to me.

"Joyce, you must copy everything I do when we get out of bed."

She followed me just as I had asked and at one point spoke, though saying simply:

"I will be going home," she said flatly.

"I am afraid to say that is what is what Sister Kilshaw says to all the new girls," I explained. "It is to get you to sleep."

This brought on another bout of crying.

Yet even so she followed me closely and copied everything I did, and she answered me with a yes or a no, but try as I might I could not get a conversation out of her,

I knew what it felt like to be extremely shy, so I persevered. While we were in the washroom I noticed how extraordinary her auburn hair was, how rich her brown eyes were and how flawless her complexion.

After breakfast Sister Devereaux called Joyce to her desk. I knew it was Sister's little talk that she gave to all the new girls.

Joyce however was sat with downcast eyes and I did not see her speak much at all in return.

It was raining heavily outside, so our walk was just around the streets. I was taller than Joyce, so she was quite far behind me in the crocodile, partnering another girl.

An opportunity for trying to open a conversation with Joyce did not arise until play hour when Joyce was sitting by herself with a pair of knitting needles and a ball of wool and so I watched her from afar.

Then I walked over to her and asked her what she was making. Without looking up she picked up her knitting pattern and passed it to me, The picture showed a matinee set for a baby doll. I handed it back, saying it was pretty, but she did not reply.

I then sat down beside her.

"I cannot knit," I said, "is it easy to learn?"

She looked up briefly.

"Yes it is," she said and then her eyes returned to her knitting.

I remained silent for a moment.

"I wish I could knit too," I said.

Joyce either did not hear me, or chose not to answer me, for the only reply was the clicking of needles.

I spike of anger rose in me, for once again I had offered her friendship and once again she had refused.

I left her and I did not care if she sat forever by herself with her knitting. I was finished with her and there was no way I was going to try to make conversation with her ever again.

The following day she complied with the nurses' demands and agreed to cough into the bowl, but once again there was no conversation. Although she stuck to me like glue in the washroom she did not make even the slightest effort to reply to me when I spoke to her. I was getting tired of trying with Joyce. I had been shy when I had been admitted but I had not shunned Christine's help and friendship, so that the difference between Joyce and I was getting wider.

Joyce was ignoring me to the point of rudeness.

On the fourth morning after her arrival a feeling of resentment towards her had started to bubble up within me. Why was I continuing to make an effort when it was so obvious that she did not like me? So that morning I did not talk to her at all.

We queued for the washroom in silence, washed ourselves and cleaned our teeth in silence, and neither of us spoke as we parted company and took our places in the queue for the dining room.

That evening during play hour and before bedtime Flora and Rebecca invited me to join them in their play but I said I felt like reading a book, so with my doll beside me I got myself comfortable and began reading. I was an avid reader but I found I could not concentrate because my eyes were drawn to Joyce, who, as I observed, was once again sitting alone and knitting.

Rebecca interrupted my observations.

"Come and play," said Rebecca excitedly, "I have just received a wonderful stencil set from my parents, "and look, Flora is joining in."

Then Rebecca also looked towards Joyce.

"Will Joyce come?" she asked.

I sighed.

"Joyce has made it plain to me that she does not like me very much, or anyone else for that matter."

I joined my friends and then it was Flora that studied the lone knitter.

"She's homesick," said Flora and then she readied herself, "I will ask her to play with us," she said.

I watched Flora walk over to Joyce and I saw Joyce shake her head, so that Flora came back alone and rejoined Rebecca and myself.

"I knew she would refuse us," I said spitefully. "Anyway, " I said with more than a little exasperation, "she would spoil the fun."

I was finding Joyce extremely irritating and my dislike of her was growing by the hour.

My band of friends were making pictures with Rebecca's stencil set and then we began colouring and painting.

Then out of the corner of my eye I noticed Sister had interrupted Joyce's knitting by calling her over to her desk and then speaking with her. I was mildly curious about what was being said and whether Sister had noticed Flora's futile attempt to be friendly with her.

The following evening I chose again to sit quietly reading a book and again with my dolly beside me. I was missing Christine in so many ways and was wishing she had not gone home before me. Flora and Rebacca were my good friends, but even they seemed to have changed without the steadying influence of Christine. We had been a foursome but now we were a triangle, and often I felt a bit left out. Christine had been our counsellor in troubled times, our navigator in moral dilemmas.

I spent the rest of playtime with my head full of solemn thoughts, and I was relived when the order for bedtime came.

When I arose Sister Devereaux called me over to her desk.

"I want to talk with you about the new patient, Joyce Woodhead."

My face immediately assumed a sullen expression.

Then after waiting to to see if I had any to say on the subject, Sister resumed.

"I rather thought that you and Joyce might become friends, especially as you occupy adjacent beds."

I was silent for a moment.

Then deciding honesty was the best policy, I spoke.

"I don't like her, Sister," I said.

Sister studied me.

"Why don't you like her?"

I sighed.

"Because when I try to talk to her she just rudely ignores me," I said, "and so I am also ignoring her too."

"That is a very uncharitable attitude to take, Eleanor," she said, "I am very disappointed in you. Surely you remember how Christine helped you in the early days?"

I did not reply. I felt resentful that Sister was finding fault with me when I had tried my very best.

She continued.

"Has it occurred to you that her rudeness, as you put it, might simply be her shyness? Perhaps she has difficulty talking to people she does not know?

I remained silent.

Sister however, did not.

Sister's voice became stern.

"I think you have an unhelpful attitude, Eadie, and it is high time you mended your ways."

Her sudden change of mood startled me, for I could see anger in her eyes. My resentment was suddenly overshadowed by the fear and awe of Sister's wrath,

"I am not asking you," she said, "I am *ordering* you to offer the hand of friendship to Joyce. I shall be watching you closely, Eadie. That is all!"

Chapter 29.

During our morning walk my head was full of thoughts of how Sister Devereaux had wrongly accused me of being unfriendly, and saying I had a poor attitude. If anyone one had a poor attitude it was Joyce and could Sister not see that? My blood coursed through my veins as I mulled over her remarks, I felt she had totally misjudge me.

My foul mood lasted through the day. Playtime came, and once again Joyce sat on her own with her knitting. Although Sister Devereaux did not appear to looking at me I knew for certain that she was, and no doubt waiting for me to make the first move in breaking the ice with Joyce.

To refuse to obey Sister's command would land me firmly in her bad books, so, with my dolly in my arms I walked over to Joyce and sat down beside her and watched her knit for a moment or two. Although I did not like her, I envied her ability to knit and wished I could do the same, so I spoke.

"I want to be able to knit too," I said, "can you teach me how to do it?"

She looked up and to my utter surprise she spoke.

"You need a pair of knitting needles and some wool," she said.

I thought about this.

"Then I shall write home and ask my mam and dad to send me some," I said brightly.

My further attempts to talk to her failed, and there was an awkward silence.

I glanced across at Sister's desk, but she seemed oblivious to us. Nevertheless I did not dare to return to my seat, so I tried to think of something that would grab Joyce's attention.

Inspiration came.

"I will be visiting day a week on Saturday. Are you looking forward to seeing your mummy and daddy?"

She did not reply and simply stared down at her knitting needles.

I tried again.

"I can remember my first visiting day. It was wonderful to see my mam. We were so happy to see each other," I said.

I had now succeeded in getting Joiyce's full attention, for she was looking straight at me, and as I looked I saw a deep sadness and she had tears that she was desperately trying to hold back.

Joyce was hurt and perhaps too shy to express how she felt to anyone. How could I have been so blind? I, of all people, should have understood the agonies of finding conversation with people almost impossible!

Then guided by my understanding, I knew exactly what to do.

Putting down my dolly aside I slid closer to her on the bench and then putting my arms around her I hugged her so tightly that she could not have escaped my embrace even if she wanted to. I felt her whole body shudder, followed by a huge sob, and then her tears flowed.

I sat there holding her, whilst explaining my own predicament.

"My best friend went home last week," I said. "Although I have other friends I no longer have a best friend."

I released her, perhaps appreciating there was no one now to hug me.

"Perhaps we can become each other's best friends," I said, as Joyce mopped her tears.

Then for the first time since she had entered the hospital she smiled.

From that day on, playtime saw Joyce and I sitting together and talking. As I slowly gained her confidence she explained how she had always found it difficult to talk to other children.

"I have never had a best friend before," she explained to me.

"I know just what that is like," I said, "I used to be shy - actually I was just as shy as you."

Joyce enjoyed reading and had many classic children's books. We had other things in common too, such as drawing and painting and I found myself warming to this quiet and thoughtful girl now that she had overcome her shyness. Yet even so, she clung to me like a limpet. Wherever I went, Joyce was never far behind.

Then Sister decided that we should sit together at dinner and partner each other on walks, despite the slight difference in our heights.

I had written home requesting some knitting needles and at last they arrived. Joyce cast on some stitches for me, which I thought would have been easy, for I had watched her so carefully, but alas I found it very difficult. I toiled and toiled but I could not get the hang of holding the knitting needles correctly in my hands. I found I could not put the wool around without releasing and losing my grip on the needle, so that a stitch would be dropped.

I became exceedingly exasperated with my inability to do what Joyce found so easy, and my hands became sweaty with intense concentration, which made my efforts even harder. Joyce tried her best, but she was no teacher, and at the end of a long struggle I burst into tears.

Sister Devereaux, although absorbed in her paperwork, soon called me over to see what was wrong.

When I sobbed out the reason for my anguish she consoled me.

"Eleanor, I shall teach you how to knit."

Thereon, each evening, apart from when she was off duty. I approached Sister's desk. She placed a chair at the side of her and devoted ten minutes of her time to patiently instructing me on how to knit. I was taught the correct way to hold the needles, how to thread the wool through the fingers of my right hand to ensure constant tension of every stitch. She taught me how to pull the wool around without talking my hand off the needle, and I was to keep repeating to myself '*Needle in, wool around, pull it through, slide it off.*'

Suddenly a week or so later all her tuition bore fruit, and I could at last knit!

As a reward for my efforts Sister came in one day with a paper bag with some oddments of different wool inside and she suggested I knit a multi-coloured scarf.

I now felt on par with Joyce, for I too was knitting something and every playtime saw us knitting together and chattering and our friendship became firm and deep.

Joyce was quiet and studious, and preferred to listen to what others had to say rather than join in, and it took some time before she was at ease with Flora and Rebecca, though in fact she never achieved the closeness with them that she enjoyed with me. She was perfectly happy to have just one friend, namely myself.

Chapter 30.

May gave way to June with all the delights that summer brings. The dark days were over and we were going to bed in daylight.

Uppermost in every girl's thoughts in Fortitude Ward were the upcoming medicals that would take place at the end of the month. I had been a patient in the hospital since the end of October 1947, a period of nearly eight months. Just how many more medical examinations would I fail? Sometimes I felt ike I was never going to be discharged, and yet surely the day would eventually come when I would be going home. They could not keep me here for ever and ever, could they?

In the meantime, although I was homesick. I was not unhappy either. For one thing I had Nurse Owens. I now absolutely idolised her, not only because she was very pretty, but also because she was so kind and loving to us all. I wanted to be really special to her and began trying to attract her attention at every opportunity. I even tried (unsuccessfully) to speak like her, and I studied her mannerisms and tried to copy them. I was obsessed with her, and I thought she was the loveliest nurse in the whole world. If she ever had to rebuke me for something (which was not often) then I would be inconsolable.

One day she took to fondly calling me 'Pansy' - a nickname I liked, until the following day she extended the name to 'Pansy Potter.' I immediately thought she was seeing me as a comic character and was in tears. She comforted me, unaware that I had placed her on an imaginary pedestal that was ten feet high.

I also liked Nurse Mollett very much, for she was hardworking and very caring. She was always hugging and kissing us, especially if she thought we were in need of a little bit of loving. But I did not hero-worship her in the way I did Nurse Owens. There were many nurses, too numerous to mention in any detail. They were all caring and loving, but these were my two special favourites.

I was also enjoying my friendship with Joyce. It was now hard to imagine that I had at first disliked her, for we were now inseparable and perfectly happy in each other's company. Her shyness with me had disappeared completely. We were never short of things to talk about, for conversation came easily for both of us.

On visiting days Joyce's mother began coming over to me before she said her goodbyes, and she always gave me a kiss and had a brief chat with my mam. This deepened our friendship even further. During one visit Joyce's mother mentioned me to my mam:

"I am so pleased that Joyce and Eleanor have become such good friends, Mrs Eadie," she said. "Me and my husband were ever so worried about Joyce coming here because, well - she does not talk."

As well as Joyce of course I had Flora and Rebecca. I especially valued Flora's friendship, for she had been my friend right from day one. She was so full of fun, she radiated happiness and it was impossible not to smile when Flora was around, even if I was feeling a little glum. I liked Rebecca too, and wondered what people would make of her when she finally went home. She had completely changed since being in the hospital. I often wondered what had brought about her change of character but I was unable to come up with an answer. The only thing I knew for sure was that I greatly valued her friendship.

It was on a sunny day in June 1948 that we took a morning walk on the promenade. At first I felt a stab of envy when I saw children enjoying themselves with their parents, but it was a fleeting emotion and I soon got used to the holidaymakers having a good time. Unlike the local people, tourists did now know who we were or where we came from. They would stand and watch us go by - a crocodile of girls, all dressed in navy blue with a nurse at the front and rear.

That morning was a beautiful morning and I felt happy as I walked along the prom with Joyce beside me. We leaned over the promenade railings and saw the water was absolutely teeming with jellyfish. We stood pondering just how many there were. It would have been impossible for a bather to put their toe in the water without getting stung.

Flora came up to us, her eyes glittering as she hopped excitedly around, urging us to look ahead to where she was pointing.

When I looked I could not believe my eyes.

In the distance there was a fairground.

Flora ran to the nurses, imploring them to allow us to take a look at the fairground rides. The nurses agreed, so we all began walking as fast as we could towards that colourful distant scene. The sound of the organ music was getting louder as we got nearer. It was a travelling fair with a man dressed smartly greeting everyone who passed by.

Our crocodile caught the attention of the showman and he came along to talk to the nurses, who told him who we were and where were from. Meanwhile we had all turned and were staring at the wonder of the fair.

I had seldom seen such a sight, for the war with it s blackouts had deprived so many children of such spectacles as these. I thought I was stood at the gates of Heaven as I listened to the jolly organ music and watched the sights and heard the sounds of happiness as people were laughing out loud or else screaming with excitement. Children were walking around with toffee apples and other delights and I ached with envy knowing that, for us, all the fun of the fair was to be observed from a distance.

At least that is what I thought.

After talking with the nurses the showman announced that every patient could have a ride on his gondolas absolutely free of charge.

The gondolas were brightly painted wooden swings that held two people seated facing each other, and each person in turn had to pull on a colourful rope with a bright tassel on the end to have the gondola swing. The harder one pulled the higher the gondola went, and those who became synchronised and in rhythm could make them swing high.

Oh what a scramble there was to be first on a swing! I climbed into a gondola with Joyce and together we swung higher and higher. I felt as if we would touch the sky as my as the wind tugged at my clothes and hair. I had never experienced such exhilaration. Afterwards we all lined up and said "*Thank you*," in unison to the showman.

"It has been my very great pleasure," he said roundly.

We were all so happy, chattering excitedly about our treat as we walked back to the hospital.

What a perfect morning it had been. Life felt so wonderful, I thought to myself. Even if I failed my medical and had to spend the rest of the summer in the hospital then I would not have cared if every day had been like today.

Joyce was excited too.

"I am so happy now," she said, "I keep praying that you will not go home before me."

Adding to my happiness was the fact that I had not been in trouble with Sister for some time.

"Everything will be fine, " I said merrily, "if I am careful and I do not do anything to make Sister cross," I said.

Flora heard me and she grinned.

"You will not keep it up for long!" she called.

"You might be wrong, you know," I said.

Flora found this most amusing.

"I shall be watching," she said. "Oh yes I will!"

"You might have a long wait," I said.

However, Flora could not have made a more accurate prediction, for my troubles began that very night.

Chapter 31.

At night the corridor lights were dimmed and left on for the duration of the night, and this was a draw for moths and various creepy crawlies of the night, which were drawn to the lamps and or else to the shelter and the stillness.

I awoke in the early hours of the morning and I slowly looked out and then I froze, for directly in my vision were two luminous eyes staring at me unblinkingly. I was terror stricken - a gorilla standing on my bed could not have generated more fear in me.

I let out a scream that a banshee would have been proud of.

Every girl in Fortitude Ward was suddenly awake, some also screaming, since panic is easily spread.

Sister Kilshaw came hurrying in to see what was to do, and clicking on the lights they revealed my 'monster' was only a very large moth that had settled on my pillow. Sister Kilshaw disturbed it and it flew away, but it left a powdery substance from its wings on my pillow where it had rested.

Sister Kilshaw and the night nurse then found themselves in charge of a ward of wide-awake patients who could not go back to sleep. Then, having been rudely awoken, every girl asked to go to the toilet. The girls had to be taken four at a time to the washroom. I was feeling extremely anxious, for I knew all of this hullabaloo would be reported to Sister Devereaux in the morning and that I would be summoned to her desk. I knew she would be very cross with me, and I gave great thought to what I would say when I was stood in front of her. I began composing what I hoped would be a perfect account of why I screamed, hoping against hope that Sister would take this into consideration.

I lay in bed rehearsing what I would say whilst tossing and turning until dawn began to break, when I at last fell asleep.

When I awoke, the moth immediately came into my mind. As I coughed and spit into the bowl I began once again running through my prepared statement.

After breakfast I was summoned to Sister's desk.

Sister never shouted but I could always tell when she was annoyed because she spoke quietly and exactly.

She leant forward and folded her arms on her desk.

"Tell me Eadie, what is a night moth?"

"It looks like," and I paused, "It looks like a butterfly, Sister."

"And what else?"

I was struggling for an answer, so I relied on my rehearsed account.

"It flies around at night, Sister, and it has huge eyes that -," but Sister stopped me before I could utter another word.

"It is patently obvious that you are familiar with night moths, and therefore your over-reaction during the night is totally inexcusable. Your unbounded hysterics brought about a traumatic night for everyone, including the night staff."

"But Sister," I began, ""I was frightened because -."

Yet again she cut me off.

"You will go to bed at six o' clock every evening for seven days, starting forthwith. You will also, in my presence, apologise to Sister Kilshaw for your unreasonable behaviour."

She paused and then added.

"I expect to hear a humble and sincere apology delivered to her by you, otherwise I shall add a further seven days. Is that understood?"

"Yes, Sister."

"You may return to your seat."

I sat down.

Then Sister addressed us all.

"Every girl in Patience and Fortitude Wards will go to bed at six o' clock this evening, for all of you contributed to the disturbance in the night. That is all."

Now I felt worse. Everyone was missing their playtime because of me. A feeling of anger was rising up within me, for Sister had not given me a chance to give my version of events on why I had been so frightened. She had not shown the slightest interest in knowing the facts, and I felt she had judged me unfairly.

That evening a nurse told me to get out of bed and to go to Patience Ward, where I found Sister Devereaux was waiting for me along with Sister Kilshaw.

I knew what was expected of me and so I said:

"I want to apologise for all the trouble I caused last night, and I will never do it again," I said.

"Apology accepted," said Sister Kilshaw, who smiled at me."

A nurse then took me back to Fortitude Ward where I climbed back into bed, and there I lay with my head full of resentment for Sister's unfairness.

Each night I lay in bed listening to the rest of the girls enjoying their playtime in the dining room, and the bitter emotions that had engulfed me added to my misery.

During the day I was rather removed from Joyce, Flora and Rebecca, preferring my own company whilst resentful thoughts festered in my head.

Every time Sister Devereaux looked at me I looked away. Not wanting to look into her eyes. I took great pains not to look anywhere near her, except when it was unavoidable such as when I was receive letters from home - when I would take th letter from her hand without looking at her.

I had mistakenly thought I had begun to understand her, and even admire her. How wrong I had been, for now I knew how cold and unfeeling she was.

On the third of my early nights I left the dining room and was walking down the corridor to get my nightdress out of my locker when I saw Dister Devereaux come out through the door of Courtesy Ward. I quickly entered Fortitude Ward, got my nightdress out of my locker but purposely took longer over the procedure than I needed to in order to allow

Sister to continue on her way. But when I eventually left Fortitude Ward I discovered Sister Devereaux had not made very much progress at all and seeing me she placed a restraining hand on my shoulder.

I froze, not looking at her.

She gently patted me on the top of my head and then reaching for my hand she spoke.

"Goodnight, Forget-Me-Not," she said.

I reluctantly looked up and she was smiling warmly at me.

All my feelings of resentment melted away as she squeezed my hand affectionately.

"Goodnight, Sister," I replied, returning her smile.

I felt that the tension of the last few days was over and the rest of that week's punishment should not be added to by my bitterness, which had poisoned me horribly. I went to bed in good spirits, at least for my own sake.

Sister had a genuine concern for the patients but also an indomitable strictness. I had tried so hard to stay out of range of her temper, but rather like a moth I had inadvertently strayed too close. Yet for all her rigidity she liked me, which made her punishments that much harder, perhaps for the both of us.

The next day I reverted to my usual self, seeing Sister Devereaux as simply a hazard, and finding comfort in the good friends that I was lucky enough to have around me.

From that week on I became acutely aware of how many moths entered our ward at night-time. I could see them in silhouette as they performed an aerial ballet, darting and diving and skittering against the corridor windows in pursuit of the light. I hated them, but never again did I scream.

Chapter 32.

My first thought one particular morning as I heard the clanking of bowls was that today was the day of the June 1948 medicals. I had now been in the hospital for eight long months, having failed two previous medicals. The thought of going home and being a part of a family again was filling me with exhilaration. There would be no more of this hated coughing on a morning. I would be be able to sleep in my own bed again, and wear my own clothes - colourful clothes: reds, yellows, pinks, greens - any colour other than navy blue.

After breakfast we were ushered down the corridor by a nurse into a waiting room where we were told to strip down to our vests and knickers and then wait for our names to be called by the doctor. Not one of us spoke as we sat fidgeting, the only sounds being our occasional coughing and the general noises of the hospital.

When it came to my turn I was weighed and I discovered I had gained back my weight plus another two pounds. The doctor then placed his stethoscope on my chest and asked me to breathe in and out. Then next he asked me to cough while he listened.

We had two weeks to wait for the medical results, and everyone was tense from anticipation of hopefully hearing good news.

Sister read out the names of the girls who were to be discharged. There were seven girls from Fortitude Ward, one of whom was Flora, who was jumping for joy. There were also patients discharged from Patience and Courtesy Wards.

My name was not read out.

I was bitterly disappointed and I envied Flora, whom I knew I would dearly miss when she had gone home. Would my turn ever come? I felt like a prisoner doomed to remain within these walls forever.

Joyce did not voice her thoughts, but she was clearly relieved that she was not going to lose her friend.

It was emotional goodbye to Flora, for she had been one of my very best friends in the hospital, but Rebecca found saying goodbye heart-breaking, as she waved goodbye to her very best friend.

A little later I saw Sister talking to Rebecca and holding her hand, and I knew Sister was comforting her.

Over the next few days new patients were admitted who replaced those who had gone home. By the end of the week the disruption was over. I counted up how many girls had gone home during my stay and I counted twelve. A girl had been discharged last January, plus two more in March, then there were Dorothy and Christine, and now seven girls had gone home this month. Therefore only five of the original Fortitude Ward companions remained. Thankfully Rebecca found herself a new friend named Lily Beddows.

One of the shoe cleaners had gone home, and I decided I wanted to be a shoe cleaner. The shoe cleaners worked in the period following our afternoon walk when girls would queue up in the corridor waiting for the bath or showers. Shoe cleaners had the luxury of bathing last and longest. I also knew very well that shoe-cleaners could hear the conversations of nurses as they strolled along the path outside, and that was another reason why I wanted the job.

After breakfast that morning I approached Sister Devereaux's desk, asking for permission to speak.

After receiving Sister's permission I explained myself.

"Please, Sister, I would like to be a shoe-cleaner," I said.

"A shoe-cleaner," Sister said and half-smiled. She raised an eyebrow.

"How do I know you are capable of doing the job well?"

Then she paused for thought, then her smile suddenly broadened.

"I want you to fetch the shoe shine box from the washroom and clean my shoes. If you make a good job of them then you can be a shoe-cleaner."

I went along to the washroom and picked up the shoe shine box and returned to Sister. I placed the box on the floor and then kneeling down beside her I waited for her to take off her shoes. She did not take off her shoes and instead she stuck out her right foot, and when I still did not move she said:

"Well, get on with it then!"

I then realised that she was expecting me to shine her shoes while they were on her feet. I felt annoyance that she was purposefully making it difficult for me, but regardless of this I began.

I opened the black polish and carefully applied it to to her shoe, taking care not to brush her stockings. Then with equal care I brushed the polish off. Then finally I buffed up a shine with the duster. She held up her foot to inspect my work, and then stuck out her left foot.

I repeated the process.

Whilst I was busy brushing, Nurse Mollett came into the dining room and I glanced up at her. She did not say a word but her expression silently queried what I was doing.

In answer to Nurse Mollett's unspoken question, Sister explained.

"Eleanor wants to be a shoe-cleaner!" she said.

I looked up at Sister at this point and saw she was laughing, and saw that Nurse Mollett's eyes were full of merriment too.

When I had finished my work Sister inspected her shoes.

She gently raised my chin with her fingers.

"Well done, Forget-Me-Not, you are now a shoe-cleaner," and she smiled, still with laughter in her eyes.

This was the second time that Sister had revealed she had a sense of humour, the first being when she had re-labelled my comb. The bizarre ritual of the shoes, which caused her to laugh, had me warming to her in a way that I would never have thought possible when I had first entered the hospital.

Chapter 33.

Sister Devereaux's section of the hospital had a capacity for thirty six patients: eighteen in Fortitude Ward, nine in Patience Ward and nine in Courtesy. Rarely was every bed in Courtesy Ward occupied, because a couple of beds were reserved for emergencies to allow for a reshuffle if a Fortitude girl was taken ill. Patients from all three wards, who were well enough, ate together in the dining room. I knew everyone's names, but never got friendly with the older and younger ones because we tended to separate into three main age groups. The groups were: five to age year olds, nine to eleven year olds and twelve to fourteen year olds.

Joyce had not liked it when she learned I had applied to be a shoe-cleaner, for it meant she would be queuing for the bathroom on her own. However my decision had been made and for sound reasons. Firstly it was considered an honour to be a shoe-cleaner, and secondly a shoe-cleaner would be able to pass on first hand any information I overheard. Just as I had relied on the shoe-cleaners in the past then others would now rely on me.

The day following the shoe-cleaning episode with Sister, Nurse Mollett took me into the washroom where Connie Dixon and Olwyn Jones were waiting. They were both fourteen year olds. Connie was in Courtesy Ward. Olywn was in Fortitude. I did not know either of them very well but they both smiled, and Nurse Mollett asked them to make me welcome and to show me what to do. As she was leaving she placed a wedge under the washroom door to keep it open, and explained to me that Sister liked staff to be able to see patients at all times, and the door must never be closed while we were shoe-cleaning.

Connie and Olywn had responsibility for brushing on the polish buffing up a shine, whilst I was given the task of brushing the polish off. We all three sat on the floor whilst shoes were taken from the rack and cleaned, taking care that right shoes and left shoes were kept together. The shoes were then kept in the rack with no semblance of order, for everyone knew their own shoes, regardless of where they were positioned.

I was sat in the middle whilst Connie and Olwyn chatted to each other, since they knew each other very well. They talked about things that either did not interest me or else I did not understand. On occasions when I spoke in response to some topic they would stop talking and silence me with meaningful looks, then carry on with their conversation. Therefore I gave up trying to join in and concentrated on cleaning the shoes.

When all the shoes were cleaned Connie and Olwyn stood up and explained that the new girl cleared up. They left me alone to put the tins of polish, brushes and dusters away in the shoe-shine box. I then made my way to the bathroom where the two other shoe-shiners were already in the showers, so I filled the bath and got in. I had not enjoyed the shoe-cleaning at all, and what's more I had not heard one single nurse talking outside the window.

I had previously queued in line for the bathroom, and the queue always began with the eldest at the front and the little ones at the back, therefore my fellow bathers were always around my age. I was therefore shocked when Connie and Olwyn emerged naked from the showers and showed they were both fully developed, for I had never seen a naked female with breasts before and I was dreadfully embarrassed. I lowered my eyes but I could still see them through the corners of my eyes chatting and laughing.

I picked up my flannel and put it over my face, completely blocking my vision. I could hear them talking about film stars they admired. I lay with my eyes covered until Nurse Mollett told me to stop messing about and get out of the bath. When I removed the flannel I was so relieved to see the girls now had towels about them. Nurse Mollett dried me and helped me get dressed, combed my hair and then I went into the dining room for teatime.

Joyce was pleased to see me.

"Did you like shoe-cleaning?" she asked.

"Yes," I said, but inwardly I was not sure. I felt I had made a big mistake, yet how could I admit this to Sister when I had specifically asked to be a shoe-cleaner?

The following day was Wednesday and Staff Nurse Briggs was one duty, for it was Sister's day off, and I so could not have voiced my reservations even if I had wanted to.

When shoe-cleaning time came around and I was to brush the polish off once again I felt some frustration.

Finally I spoke.

"I was told we took it in turns and I would not be doing one thing each time," I said.

"We are older than you," Connie said, "you have to do as we say. Are you going to go snivelling to Sister?"

Then Connie turned to Olwyn.

"No one likes a tell-tale, do they, Olwyn?"

Olwyn merely smiled.

"But we are supposed to take turns," I explained again.

Connie became annoyed and was glaring at me.

"You will do as you are told," she said, "otherwise you will regret it."

Then as I watched her it seemed that an idea came into her head.

She pointed at the toilet.

"You will go sit on the toilet and use it."

I did not want to go to the toilet but Connie's face made me change my mind, so I went over to the toilet and made ready and sat on it.

Connie was now enjoying herself.

"You are not to move until you are done," she said.

I sat there no matter what.

I sat there but no matter how I tried I could not use the toilet as she demanded.

She held one finger up.

"Worse will happen to you if you dare to stand up!"

The look on Connie's face suggested she was deriving some sadistic pleasure from seeing me so distressed.

She then crawled across the floor and put her head between my legs.

"I still cannot hear anything!"

By this time I was becoming very upset and was beginning to cry whilst wondering just what was to come next.

To my great relief a passing nurse glanced through the door.

"Connie!" the nurse said, "what are you doing?"

I quickly stood up and redressed myself and Connie and I returned to our shoe-cleaning duties.

Connie glared at me.

"I am not finished with you," she whispered. "There will be more of the same to come later."

I was quaking with fear.

So this was how it was to be. I was at the mercy of bullies, and I knew that there was nothing I could do about it. They were older than me and they were two against one.

I did not want to be a shoe cleaner any more.

I continued brushing the polish off the shoes and remained quiet, but whilst observing my fellow shoe-cleaners I noticed that Olwyn had not supported Connie but said nothing. Perhaps she did not dare to stand up to Connie any more than I did.

Olwyn Jones was in Fortitude Ward and she sometimes told us stories during talking-time before sleep. I had thought she was a nice girl, since she smiled a lot, but I was obviously wrong. Olwyn was fourteen years old, had mousy coloured straight hair and bluish grey eyes. She was Welsh and bi-lingual, being able to speak both languages fluently.

Connie Dixon was in Courtesy Ward, and prior to shoe-cleaning I had known only a little about her. I had regularly seen her seated at mealtimes with the older girls, but I had never spoken to her. She had dark brown hair and brown eyes. Her forehead was narrow and hairline grew into what was commonly known as a 'widow's peak.' Her teeth were crooked and she had a slight lisp when she spoke. But for all her misfortunes I could find no sympathy for her and I disliked her intensely.

Once again and after next shoe-shining duty I was left to put the polish, brushes and dusters away into the shoeshine box. After this and whilst in the bath I simply tried not to look at their nudeness.

I entered the dining room, and I needed to tell someone how I was feeling, so I revealed all to Joyce, who listened to every word. She was so upset to hear I was so unhappy.

"Are you going to tell Sister that you want to give up shoe-cleaning?"

"I cannot do do that," I said, "because Sister will want to know why and she would not stop until she got the truth out of me. I cannot tell on Connie and Olwyn because of what they might do."

Joyce had a think.

"Well Connie is in Courtesy Ward and she might be going home soon," she said. "If she goes home I will ask to be a shoe-cleaner too."

Joyce was right. Courtesy girls did not stay long, so I could perhaps try to stick it out until Joyce could hopefully join me.

The following day (Thursday) Sister was back on duty, and after breakfast she called me over to her desk.

"How are you getting on as a shoe-cleaner?" she asked. "Are there any problems?"

I intertwined the fingers of my hands and looked at them.

Here was a perfect opportunity to tell her about Connie, but I found I could not. I was convinced that the rest of the girls would frown on me from 'telling' on another, and so I kept my own counsel.

"No Sister," I said, "there are no problems."

I waited for her to dismiss me but she did not speak.

I shifted the positions of my fingers and then untwined them, then finally I clasped my hands together.

Her silence was now beginning to make me feel uncomfortable, so I raised my gaze and looked at her.

At this she sat forward in her chair. An elbow was placed on the desk and her chin was cupped in her palm and her eyes were fixed on me.

I lowered my gaze again.

She finally spoke.

"Don't you like me, Eleanor?" she asked.

Her words caused me to look up at her in surprise.

"I do," I replied.

"Then why is it that when I ask you a question you do not look me in the eye?"

I was trying desperately to think of something to say.

However Sister continued.

"I think there is something you are not telling me. Am I right?"

I shook my head.

Sister sat back.

"Very well," she said, "you may go."

I walked away feeling uneasy. What if she questioned Connie and Olwyn? Then if they suspected that I had told on them it might make matters worse. My mind was in turmoil. Such being the power of the bully, as too many of us know.

Our morning walk was to the rock pools, which was now one of my favourite places.

The sun on my face, the wind in my hair and the feeling of being at one with Nature cast out all of my anxiety. Joyce, now a fellow observer of the theatre of those little watery worlds, was as keen to peer into the little depths as I was.

In the afternoon we walked to Willows Hill and Joyce and I went right to the top where there were the seats for people to sit stare. As we approached I noticed a small item on one of the seats so I went over to see what it was.

It was a one penny coin.

I held it in my hand.

This was the first time in nearly nine months that I had held a coin of the realm, and it made me realise just how out of touch I was with the outside world. Handling pocket money at home had become a distant memory. The coin had Brittania on the tails side and the head of King George VI on the reverse. What use was this coin to me? Yet I prized my find and slipped the penny into my pocket to remind me of pre-hospital days.

Upon returning to the hospital my exhilaration was dampened a little by the thought of having to join Connie and Olwyn for shoe-cleaning. I walked into the washroom with a heavy heart and saw Connie and Olwyn were waiting.

Olwyn smiled.

"It is your turn for buffing, " she said as she handed me the duster.

Amazed I took the duster from her hand and we sat down on the floor and we began our work.

Connie and Olwyn chatted with each other as usual, whilst I remained silent.

All through the shoe-cleaning Connie did not say anything to me - not one word. Olwyn however spoke to me often and smiled. They even helped in putting the shoe cleaning equipment back into the shoe-shine box.

Whilst Connie made no attempt to be friendly, she no longer tormented me, and so my thoughts turned to my conversation with Sister Devereaux that morning, and I remembered how she investigated matters to exhaustive lengths.

I considered it a compete mystery how Sister knew when a child was telling a lie, and I had begun to assume that she possessed magical powers or else she could somehow read our minds.

Connie never bullied me again.

Then over the next few weeks I became friendly with Olwyn. I was fascinated by the fact that she could speak Welsh, and she spent time trying to teach me a few Gaelic words. 'Hello,' was '*Helo,*' which was very much the same, while 'Goobye,' was '*Hwyl fawr,*' which had a lovely tone to it. '*Nos da,*' was 'Goodnight.'

I was happy again.

I was further relieved when a few weeks later Connie reached her 15th birthday and was transferred to an adult hospital, and Joyce successfully applied to be a shoe-cleaner. The shoe-cleaning sessions were now pleasurable. Furthermore we regularly heard nurses chatting to each other while walking on the path outside the washroom. For a long time there was just general chit-chat. Then there came news that left us with gaping mouths.

Nurse Owens was talking to another nurse about an exam she had recently taken, and that she was hoping she would pass, for she would be qualified to apply for a post at Liverpool Royal Infirmary.

Joyce, Olwyn and I stared at each other in dismay, for we adored Nurse Owens. During playtime we reported our eavesdropping to the rest of the girls. Everyone who heard was feeling downhearted at the prospect of Nurse Owens leaving. As for myself, and quite selfishly, I hoped secretly that Nurse Owens would fail her exam, so that she would stay with us.

Chapter 34.

The next day was a tremendous day that came quite unexpectedly, for after mealtime Sister called for our attentions.

"There are sufficient donations available to give you another treat," she said.

"Tomorrow the seven to fourteen year olds will be having a day out in Liverpool. You will be visiting the cathedral and perhaps have a walk around the city if time permits," she said. "You will be taking a packed lunch with you and you will be served a hot meal when you return to the hospital."

Then she turned to the younger ones.

"The five to six year olds will be taken to a local farm where there is a pets' corner and where you will be able to touch the animals."

At this there were whoops of joy from the youngest patients.

I went to bed that night, not only thinking about the forthcoming trip to Liverpool, but also excited at being free from the monotonous daily routine of the hospital. Every day we knew exactly what we would be doing at any given time, even the meals were a weekly set menu and never varied. The only variation each day was where we walked, and although some of the walks were pleasurable they did tend to become commonplace as the months went by. Scenery that had once caught my eye now went by unnoticed.

After breakfast Sister handed us all a typed sheet giving us the history of Liverpool and details of the Cathedral. A motor coach had been ordered to transport us to Birkenhead, and we all climbed aboard.

This was indeed a treat, for I could not remember the last time I had been on a motor coach. Normally we would have been setting off on our morning walk. Joyce and I sat together and I watched scenery flick by that we had never seen before. It was such a change from our repetitive walks and I wondered if those kind people who had given money to the hospital had any idea how much pleasure they were giving to us.

As we crossed the River Mersey by ferryboat we had a wonderful view of Liverpool's miles of waterfront, where the famous Liver Building was topped by the statues of the birds, popularly known as The Liver BIrds.

When we arrived in Liverpool we were taken to the cathedral, and the first thing I noticed was all the scaffolding. We were told that construction had begun in 1904 and it would be many years before it was completed, especially as German bombs had damaged it during the recent war.

We were given a guided tour and everything was explained to us. Although unfinished I could nevertheless appreciate the grandeur of the building. Although I did not understand many of the things that were being explained to me it did not spoil my enjoyment. While I was walking around I said a little prayer inside my head asking God to please let me go home again.

When our tour of the cathedral was over the nurses took us to a little park where our lunches were distributed. We were each given a pack of sandwiches and a drink of orange juice. Then we either sat on park benches or else on the grass and enjoyed our al fresco meal.

The nurses said there was a little more time to spare before boarding the ferry and would we like to walk around the streets of the city for a while.

We all shouted: "Yes please!" in our usual fashion.

We found it enormously enjoyable to look in shop windows, especially sweet shop where jars and jars of sweets and chocolate bars were on display in the window. Even the smallest bars of chocolates were 2 ration points and cost at least four pennies each, so that even if I had thought to take the penny I had recently found I could still not have been able to afford anything. We each pressed our faces against the shop window and looking longingly at what we could not have.

Instead I began to look at the buildings' neon signs that were everywhere. Some were advertising products while others formed the names of shops, and the signs were many shapes and colours. Some signs were flashing and gave the indication of movement, which fascinated me.

I looked for the railway station but I could not see it. One day I would be here and I would visit the railway station again and a train would take me home. It was now July 1948, and the next medicals were in September. I thought of the clothes I used to wearand compared them to the fashions of the day, and decided that when I eventually reached home I never wanted to wear anything like a uniform again.

Our walk around the city was soon over. We made our return journey on the ferry and at Birkenhead ferry port the motor coach was waiting for us. We returned to the hospital and just as was promised a hot meal was waiting for us, which was very welcome after our long day.

Chapter 35.

Three days went by and we heard no more news about Nurse Owens, so we all presumed she must have failed her exam.

On the Wednesday morning Sister Devereaux announced that she would be taking one week's holiday the following week and that Staff Nurse Briggs would be in charge.

"Any misdemeanours while I am away shall be dealt with upon my return," she said. "You must all bear this in mind and be good for Staff Nurse Briggs."

"*We will*," we all chanted in return.

On the Saturday almost everyone was in a celebratory mood because Sister was absent, and would be for a whole week. No one cared that Staff Nurse Briggs tended to shout, or even bellow to get our attention, because despite this she was far more lenient. When Sister would enter the dining room on a morning she would walk in so gracefully and bid us all good morning in her quiet refined way. Staff Nurse Briggs bustled in hastily without a trace of elegance and spoke rather bossily in a loud voice.

During the morning temperature and medication and hair combing routine Staff Nurse Briggs chatted happily with the other two nurses who who were talking about the latest songs. Yet despite the relaxed mood of the girls and nurses I still wished that it was Sister sitting here.

Sunday and Monday came and went, and then I began to miss her, for nothing seemed right without Sister Devereaux being there. Whenever I walked down the corridor I found myself looking for her, expecting her to suddenly emerge from Courtesy or Patience Ward, even though she was miles away on holiday. Instead it was Staff Nurse Briggs I saw walking up and down, but always walking quickly even when haste was not required. I could hear her quick heavy step well before she made an appearance.

Every time I entered the dining room I looked at the desk, trying to picture Sister Devereaux sitting there.

I could not understand why I missed Sister so much, and could not explain to Joyce how I felt, for she disliked Sister, and was thoroughly enjoying her absence.

"I wish she would stay away forever," Joyce said one day when she was enjoying her respite.

Many of the other girls felt the same sense of relief too, although not as deeply as Joyce.

As far as Sister's holiday was concerned it seemed that I was the only girl who was missing her.

On the Tuesday night I listened to the nurses singing in the dining room and then it was Staff Nurse Briggs who was reading a prayer. I turned over in my bed and sighed. Everything felt wrong without Sister Devereaux.

I yearned for her return.

The following morning I awoke feeling thoroughly miserable. What was wrong with me? I could not analyse why I missed Sister so much, for unlike the nurses she never demonstrated any affection and was strict with us all. It was during that week that I realised how differently I now viewed viewed Sister from when I had first been admitted. In the beginning I had hated her, loathed her with every fibre of my being. I certainly did not loathe her now. I needed her in some strange kind of way.

Joyce had become concerned about me, asking me what she had done wrong.

"Nothing," I said, then hesitated. "It is because Sister Devereaux is away and I am missing her."

Joyce stared at me with such surprise.

Then the same response came from some of the other girls when they discovered the reason for my moodiness.

Olga, someone I did not know well, seemed to speak for nearly everyone.

""I cannot imagine why you are missing Sister Devereaux; it is *so much more relaxing* with Staff Nurse Briggs in charge.

She paused for thought.

"Are you and Sister related?"

I stared at Olga.

"No, we are not," I said with surprise. "Whatever would make you say that?"

Olga shrugged her shoulders.

"Because I cannot think of another reason why you should like her so much," she said.

Following this strange conversation I hurried into the washroom and looked into the mirror. The girl looking back at me had medium brown hair, brown eyes and had teeth that were a little crooked. I had been blonde until I was five years old, and then slowly my hair had begun to darken.

Sister had blue eyes and straight teeth and our features were completely different. The only thing we had in common was the colour of our hair.

What an unusual idea Olga had. However, I was aware that I constantly tried to mimic Sister Devereaux's mannerisms and perhaps it was this that Olga had seen. I used to purposefully bite my button lip, trying to mirror her habit. Another of Sister's mannerisms was her often raising her hand sharply to flick back tresses of her hair that were not there, owing to her hair being pinned back. Yet another was evident when she was speaking to someone in the corridor. She would finish the conversation, then walk away a few steps, then stop, turn and then return to say a few more words before walking away. All of these mannerisms I had copied, without having thought about it much. It was as if I wanted to be like her.

The only person who did not notice that I was any different from my usual self was Staff Nurse Briggs. She was good at her job but was not as observant as Sister, who could tell immediately if a child was upset, even when a child was trying to hide their emotions. If I had acted like this whilst Sister was around she would have immediately demanded to know what was wrong. The only time Staff Nurse Briggs noticed when anything was wrong was when a child was shedding tears.

I was really looking forward to Monday when Sister was due to return, and the weekend before seemed endless. The feelings I was experiencing were as potent as my nostalgia for home, and just as agonising.

On the Monday morning I was awake long before the night nurse brought around the bowls. A tingling of excitement was running through me, for today Sister Devereaux would be back.

We arose and when we entered the dining-room there was Sister Devereaux seated at her desk. I wanted to run to her, but of course that was impossible. Even so I could not take me eyes off her.

Wherever Sister had been it had been sunny, for her skins was golden, giving her complexion a healthy glow.

Joyce on the other hand was bemoaning Sister's return, as were many of the other girls. However in complete contrast my days were happy again.

Joyce's dislike of Sister Devereaux reached its peak on the following visiting day at the end of July. Her mummy and daddy had booked a short holiday on the Wirral for the following week so that they could spend some time with Joyce. Joyce was absolutely delighted, but when Joyce's parents approached Sister for permission to see their daughter each day during their holiday, Sister refused their request.

Mrs Woodhead approached my mother with a face like thunder to share her frustration and disappointment and I sat listening.

"That Sister Devereaux has refused point blank to let our Joyce join us for just a few hours each day while we are here - can you believe that, Mrs Eadie!" she complained bitterly. "And while our Joyce, the poor child, was stood right there behind us when she said it!"

My mam replied.

"I certainly can believe it," she said with darkly, for just the visiting day before Mam had had a bit of an incident with Sister.

The expression of Mrs Woodhead's face indicated that she wanted to hear everything, and my mam obliged.

"Well," said my mam, "I had been travelling for hours and hours and I arrived at the hospital absolutely gasping for a cup of tea. I asked that Sister Devereaux if I could have one and she had caught me with a most awful stare and said: '*No you may not.*'

My Mother waved her hand.

"Then the woman swept passed me like she was royalty, leaving me just standing there."

Mrs Woodhead uttered a few words in commiseration.

Then my mother continued.

"That Sister Devereaux is a proper little madam, for there she was talking all hoity-toity and masterful, yet there she is just a slip of a girl."

My mam breathed a heavy sigh.

"It is like we should curtsey before her, yet all she is, Mrs Woodhead, is a glorified nurse."

Mrs Woodhead agreed.

Then my mam inquired of the reason why Joyce was denied access to her parents.

Mrs Woodhead sniffed disdainfully.

"The Sister demanded that all her patients be treated equally and that no girl could receive preferential treatment."

Mrs Woodhead gave my mam a firm look.

"We are going to take this issue right to the top. We are going to see the Matron," she said.

The conversation continued in a similar vein whilst I sat confounded.

It was as if they were talking about a different person from the Sister Devereaux I had come to know and understand so well.

Then Joyce's parents asked for and were granted an interview with Matron, who simply endorsed Sister's decision.

Joyce's mummy and daddy did not cancel their holiday, and on an evening they would stand outside the hospital and wave to Joyce as she lay in bed in Fortitude Ward.

One day however, our morning walk was on the promenade and Joyce's mummy and daddy were also there. As it was a chance meeting the nurses allowed us to play on the beach while Joyce was able to spend a little time with her parents, while the nurses turned a blind eye.

Chapter 36.

It was now August and the summer was at its height. In September there would be medicals and I felt sure that I must be due to be discharged, for by then I would have been the hospital nearly a year. It was very rare for a girl to be a patient for more than a year, so I was quite optimistic.

In the meantime shoe-cleaning duties were enjoyable, especially listening to the nurses chat to each other outside our window, at least until the day that we heard some bombshell news. Nurse Owens must have passed her exam, for we heard her telling another nurse how she had applied for a nursing post at Liverpool Infirmary and had been successful, and would be leaving the hospital.

I felt like someone had punched me in the tummy and tears stung in my eyes. My lovely Nurse Owens, whom like a number of nurses I had known for nearly a year in my young life, would be leaving. She could not leave! I thought. However, not long after Nurse Owens herself told us about her new job.

I was devastated.

The only comfort was of course the strong possibility that I might be leaving too.

September came, and there were medicals again.

I went for my medical examination with an air of confidence, for if they did not discharge me this time then I would remain a patient until the next medicals in January 1949. I felt certain no patient had ever stayed as long as that, so I was fairly confident that my stay at the hospital was over.

Once again I was wrong in my assumptions, for I was not discharged.

I could not believe it when my name was not called out from the list of girls that were going home, and neither could I hold back my tears of disappointment.

Sister Devereaux did her best to comfort me, but nothing she said could relieve my frustration at the prospect of having to stay for another three months. I felt the hospital was no longer bricks and mortar but instead a living breathing life form that had swallowed me whole and intended keeping me in within its walls forever. I felt trapped and entombed. I had seen patients arrive and go home, and yet I was still here.

Olwyn was going home. So was Rebecca, in fact every girl who had been in the hospital when I had first arrived had now left, and those that I had befriended were shortly to leave. I realised with sadness that I had now been a patient for longer than all of the girls in the three wards in Sister Devereaux's section. I fondly recalled the days when Christine and Flora and Rebecca and I had been such close friends.

Then Nurse Owens left.

On her final day she kissed us all goodbye, and what extraordinary emotional scenes there were, for everyone adored her. I was in tears and I begged her to stay because we all loved her, but her kisses, which normally acted like sticking-plasters on all emotional wounds no longer had any effect. Her last words to us all seemed to hang in the air after she had left.

"I will remember each and every one of you with fondness. I will miss you very - very much," she said.

We watched her walk down the corridor as she went off duty for the last time and watched her mingle with the boys that were hanging around at the gates.

Adding to the my melancholy was the fact that my mam and dad were having a long weekend in Southport. It was the first holiday they had had in years and I was upset because I could not go with them. It just did not seem fair that I was stuck in hospital whilst my sister would be having a good time with my mam and dad.

A girl called Rosie Edwards replaced Olwyn as shoe-cleaner. She was thirteen years old and was a patient in Fortitude Ward. She was chatty and friendly and soon settled in with Joyce and I.

As for myself I was not be discharged. I was not going on holiday. I felt miserable.

Then something happened that shook me to the very foundations of my soul.Something so heartrending and shocking that it made me feel physically ill for the whole of that day. I thought I would never get over it, since for the whole of my lifetime I had never had to face something of such magnitude, and it all began with shoes.

Shoe-cleaning was sometimes easy, and at other times difficult, depending on where we had been walking. For instance, if we had been to the rock pools and our shoes had become wet and then set hard with sand then it was more difficult to brush them clean and make them shine again. If however we had simply been on a walk through the streets on a dry day, then the shoes would merely be dusty. However, even if a pair of shoes did not appear dirty, we nevertheless cleaned them.

Then one day Rosie posed a question.

"Have either of you noticed anything strange about the shoes on the rack?"

Joyce and I looked carefully and then seeing nothing unusual we looked back at Rosie with puzzled expressions.

We could see nothing untoward whatsoever either with the rack or with the shoes that were stored on it.

Rosie continued.

"You are clearly not as observant as I am," she said and waited as Joyce and I sat with no clue as to what she meant.

Then seeing that we were not going to solve the mystery see she gave us the answer.

"One pair of those shoes never gets dirty," she explained.

It was true, and we had not noticed.

During each cleaning session we had taken down each pair of shoes and cleaned them, regardless of our own opinion of whether they needed to be cleaned or not.

Rosie held up the pair of shoes in question. I looked at them, but I did not know who they belonged to. They were about the same size as my shoes.

I stared at the others.

"I cannot think of anyone who never wears her shoes," I said.

Rosie then suggested that we place them in the top left corner of the rack and see if they moved from there. Over the coming days they never moved.

Rosie decided to ask a nurse.

Nurse Wickens had replaced Nurse Owens. She was a quick-speaking and busy nurse and she looked in on us and was approached by Rosie who explained to her the mystery of the shoes.

Nurse said she would make enquiries.

Fifteen minutes later Nurse Wickens returned, asking for the pair of shoes in question. At this we all wanted to know who the shoes belonged to.

Nurse Wickens was leaving as she replied.

"They were the shoes of a girl called Christine, who very sadly died some time ago," she said.

Upon hearing these words I felt as if a volcano was erupting inside me. Shivers went through my whole body as the full realisation of what Nurse Wickens had said pummelled me.

Rosie and Joyce knew I had been in the hospital the longest.

Rosie watched me with growing concern.

"Did you know the girl who died?"

I could not answer. My body was frozen.

I had never felt so totally shocked in my life before, for in my family, and against what might be commonly be expected, I had known no direct bereavements.

Now and very quickly everything was becoming clear to me.

I recalled the morning in Patience Ward when I awoke to see Christine's bed completely stripped down to the mattress.

Christine had died.

It had been impossible for me to conceive of death. I had believed Christine had gone home. I know understood that Christine could not leave me her favourite doll, Daisy, because Christine had died.

I finished the shoe-cleaning in a robotic fashion, making no conversation, whilst my thoughts were racing through my mind.

Christine had been ten years, like me, so how could she die? It was old people that died. Children got ill and recovered. Children could not die!

I had often heard my mam talking about elderly villagers who had died, but I had not known any of them and so their deaths had had not affected me.

I had so many unanswered questions. What had caused her to die? Then if Christine could die, then could others die too - even me?

It was all beyond what I could understand.

Later in the dining room and after teatime Sister Devereaux was very soon drawing me aside and asking me what was wrong. Under normal circumstances I would have crumbled under her scrutiny, but I was now even more confused.

Sister had let me believe that Christine had gone home. Sister had deceived me.

I closed in on myself in so complete a way that I could say nothing.

Then feeling that I should say something I told her I was missing Nurse Owens and that also my family had gone on holiday without me. These lesser troubles were finally accepted, though not entirely, as I could tell by her watchful gaze.

Without expecting it my world had turned upside down and I did not know what to do about it. I seemed to fold in on myself many times and I felt my feelings so remotely that I could not discuss my crisis with anyone, not even Joyce. Instead I was silent over Christine's death. I was a helpless vessel upon a storm of emotions. A storm of such force and duration was beginning, and I had not known its like before.

That night I lay in bed I listened to the pitter-patter of the raindrops, which seemed to my enclosed world like the sky was also crying for Christine. My grieving lasted longer within my secrecy and it was generally assumed by the other girls that my downcast mood was due to my not being discharged. In my misery there was only one comfort, which was that Christine had spent her her final hours with me, her best friend.

During the days that my parents were on holiday I felt shut out from my family and I blamed them for enjoying themselves without me. I cried when I received a postcard from them with a picture of a roller coaster. I felt taunted by their happiness.

I tore the card into little pieces.

As the weeks passed I began to think more clearly. I started to remember Sister's words following Christine's death.

"*Christine possessed many fine qualities, some of which she has passed onto you.*"

These words acted like a balm and for the first time in weeks I felt my grief was easing.

Most of all I now appreciated the support ofJoyce, who despite all of my bitter moods had remained my constant and devoted friend. There seemed no surer indication of friendship than that, no firmer proof that alongside Christine I would never forget her.

Chapter 37.

The days began to get shorter, and the nights colder. However there was still warmth in the sun, and the trees were resplendent with their autumn colours of red and gold. Berries were plentiful everywhere and it was feasting time for the birds and squirrels. During the summer months there had been the holidaymakers, but now the tourists had dwindled to just a few and these were mainly retired couples walking arm in arm.

One of our afternoon walks was along the promenade. The sun was shining and it was altogether a fine autumn day. I was still hurting following the revelation about Christine, but also genuinely appreciative of the company of Joyce, who chatted away to me, oblivious to my dark thoughts.

Most of the little wooden refreshments huts along the front were now closed and with extra shutters as preparation for the winter. However, about five hundred yards down the promenade we saw a colourful ice cream cart painted bright colours that was open. Couples who had purchased ice creams were strolling towards us licking their ice creams contentedly, and we looked on in desperation as we passed by them.

Then one of the couples stopped one of the nurses to ask who we were. At this the nurse at the rear of the crocodile went forward to join the conversation whilst we stood watching.

I tried to recall the last time I had eaten an ice cream and found it was so long ago that I could not remember where or when.

The nurses then called for our attentions and the leading nurse addressed us.

"This very kind gentleman and his wife would like to buy every one of us an icecream," she said before she was nearly deafened by a resounding roar. "So what do we say to them?" the nurse shouted.

"THANK YOU!" we all joyfully cried out and then ran as fast as we could to the ice-cream cart, whilst the elderly lady and gentleman followed on at a leisurely pace.

We were all jostling for position before the cart, each of us eager to get our hands on an ice-cream.

Eventually every girl was silently licking the delicious treat, which to me was like the food of the gods.

Oh how wonderful it was! I did not waste one single drip!

The elderly couple stood smiling, obviously deriving much pleasure from seeing us all so happy.

We were so grateful to them and after a brief discussion between ourselves we decided a chanted thank you, but then feeling this was not enough we lined up and we each of us thanked them both for their kindness.

I was not sure who was the happier, the elderly couple or us children. They bade us a cheery farewell and the nurses thanked them once again and hoped they enjoyed the rest of their holiday.

That unexpected and rather miraculous treat had helped tremendously in lifting me out of my grief. I wondered if Christine was now an angel in Heaven, perhaps like those angels painted on the ceiling in the Concert Room. Maybe she had looked down from Heaven and she had seen how happy I had been eating my ice cream!

Once again Sister Devereaux's words came into mind.

"Be happy for her knowing she has at last found the peace and contentment she was so desperately seeking."

What comfort those words gave me now.

From that day forth I did not think of Christine as being lost from us. Instead I would forever picture her as a beautiful angel full of peace and contentment and shining brightly in God's Heaven.

Chapter 38.

September gave way to October, and soon it would be my birthday. I would be eleven years old. I looked back on my tenth birthday that I had celebrated just one week before I had entered the hospital, and it seemed such a long time ago.

I tried to picture what home would look like now. Mam told me they had distempered the walls in the kitchen and also in the living room and they had bought a new rug for the kitchen floor. My sister was now six years old and doing well at school, but I wondered how well she remembered me.

Today was visiting day, and it was my dad who was was coming to see me. I was waiting eagerly to hug him and kiss him. His spine had, amazingly, righted itself and he now walked without the aid of a surgical boot. How healthy he looked as he walked into the dining room.

He told me that he and my mother plans.

"As soon as you come home from the hospital I will be looking for a job, Eleanor. I will return to being a tuner in the mill again," which I had long come to know was a highly skilled job.

"If I am successful, Eleanor, we will sell the shop as a going concern and then we shall look for a nicer house, one with a bathroom. There will no no more damp and your mother can have a quieter life."

In my turn I told him about my life in the hospital.

"I really like Sister Devereaux, Daddy," I said, "but Mam does not like her at all," I explained.

Dad was very calm and measured as usual.

"I don't want you to worry your head about that," he said. "When you are discharged we shall arrange for someone to cover at the shop and then we shall all visit here then *both* of us, your mother and I, shallthank Sister for everything she has done."

I was relieved to hear this.

"Also," I said. "Do you think Sister Devereaux is a *'proper little madam,'* because that is what Mam called her."

"Good grief, no," he said. Then he thought for a moment.

"I do not as a rule assume assume people are something they are not," he said. "And your Sister Devereaux, I can tell you, is genuine. When I was in the army I came across many people of high rank who spoke just like she does."

"Then you like her too?" I asked.

"Yes," he said. "She has always been very polite and friendly with me."

After visiting day life days in the hospital resumed their normal pattern.

The next day was BORING Sunday, dominated by church, chapel and religious instruction. No singing other than hymns. No playing with toys or games. Laughter had to be subdued. There was not even any shoe-cleaning on Sundays. Matron insisted that the Sabbath should be strictly observed in the hospital.

On this particular Sunday it was even worse, for Joyce and I got into trouble for laughing in Church.

I, along with other girls of the same faith, attended the Church of England every Sunday afternoon. We all sat on the right side of the church, and always on the same pew, accompanied by two nurses. On the left side were the boys, accompanied by a nurse and Sister Rumbold, a middle aged woman with 'middle aged spread.' Sister Rumbold had heavy jowls, was thick waisted and her legs were solid and shapeless. Her hair was frizzy and turning grey and her face was rather flat.

Sister Rumbold always paid close attention to what Canon Rhodes was saying and she would sit nodding her head in agreement as he delivered his sermon.

I used to feel such pity for the boys, because Sister Rumbold seemed to have the personality of a dragon. She was perhaps, like all of the staff, very conscientious and endearing, but in my eyes she rather loomed up as something else altogether.

We had all settled ourselves down in the pew, and Joyce began reading notes in the prayer-book that related to other services. A part explained who could not marry, a brother could not marry sister, and so on. Joyce and I began to titter, and then we got giggly and were completely unaware that Canon Rhodes was waiting for us so he that could begin his service.

Canon Rhodes coughed meaningfully and we quickly realised with embarrassment that he and the entire congregation had been waiting.

Sister Rumbold was looking at us sternly, and I could not help but compare her to a bulldog as she fixed her eyes on us.

Needless to say Sister Devereaux came to hear about our behaviour and we received the penance of two early nights for laughing in church (or for being happy in church as I later came to think of it.)

The Monday was Sister's day off, with Staff Nurse Briggs taking charge. On the Tuesday Sister was back on duty.

We were busy shoe-cleaning and as we worked the smell of cigarette smoke began to to drift through the toilet and washroom windows, which meant that nurses were standing on the pathway somewhere near.

Rosie, Joyce and I stopped talking and listened.

We did not have long to wait before we heard the voice of Nurse Stubbs. At first we could not hear all she was saying because she was too far away, just the peal of laughter from the other nurses. As the nurses walked along the path then their words became clearer.

Nurse Stubbs was talking about her latest boyfriend.

"Derek is the kind of man a girl simply dreams of meeting," she said. "He is so tall that he has to duck his head to get under doorways, and all the other girls are very envious, I can tell you."

She sighed.

"He is so good looking - and his eyes, you should see his eyes!"

They all approved.

We next heard Nurse Mollett divert the conversation and became annoyed with the perennial problem of rationing.

"I am absolutely sick and fed up of the shortages," Nurse Mollet said, "especially having to mend clothes all of the time," she said. "The only way I can marry Derek in white is if I can find a second or third-hand gown that will fit me."

Joyce, Rosie and I looked at each other with raised eyebrows as we took in this bit of news.

Then another nurse pointed out that there were actually some people the rationing did not affect.

"I saw someone we know in Birkenhead yesterday wearing Christian Dior clothes."

Nurse Mollett sniffed.

"Does not sound like anyone I know," she said.

Staff Nurse Briggs, who was also present, urged the nurse to reveal who it was.

After taking a deep breath the nurse spoke.

"It was Sister Devereaux," she said, which caused a gasps all round.

"She was wearing the '*New Look*' that Dior brought out in Paris. Wearing her hair long under a wide hat, she was, and her shoes were definitely Italian and very sleek too."

The nurse then paused for effect.

"How can she afford high fashion on a Sister's salary?" she asked the others.

Another nurse spoke.

"Perhaps she has a rich boyfriend," she ventured.

Staff Nurse Briggs made measured remark.

"Or a very rich daddy," and they all laughed.

Their talk continued on the theme of clothes, but I was not listening. Instead I was sat in a daze with my shoe brush idle in my hand. Try as I might I could not conjure an image of Sister dressed up as the figure of fashion that the nurse had described.

I slowly began brushing the shoes while Rosie chatted about Nurse Mollett getting married. I was not paying much attention, for I was engrossed in thoughts about Sister Devereaux.

I had not given a moment's thought to the fact that Sister obviously led an entirely separate life outside of the hospital. I had never seen her wearing anything other than her starched blue and white uniform with black stockings and flat black shoes. I had somehow regarded Sister Devereaux as something like a nun, devoted to her calling, and a uniform or something very much like it was how Sister always dressed.

When we went into the dining hall for our teatime I looked thoughtfully at Sister.

Surely she would not wear such extravagant clothes as that - or *would* she? I tried to conjure a mental image of Sister walking like a fashion model down the street, with her long hair loose down her back, but at each attempt I could only picture her in uniform.

I decided that the nurse must have seen someone who closely resembled Sister, a doppelganger, as they are sometimes called.

This thought soothed me.

I could well understand the confusion, for I made such a similar mistake when I thought I had seen Sister in Patience Ward on the night of that magical midnight kiss. My Sister Devereaux could never dress or behave like that. My Sister would always be dressed in her starched Sister's uniform and would never in the slightest way be removed from us.

Chapter 39.

On the eve of my eleventh birthday I had mixed emotions. I was excited at the thought of opening the birthday presents that I knew my dad would have brought with him the previous week and given to Sister. Yet at the same time I was having bouts of homesickness. I had never spent a birthday away from my family before. The only good fortune was that my birthday had fallen on a Saturday, and so there was no school.

I woke early to the sound of heavy rain, and saw that our beds had been pushed back as near to the corridor windows as possible and that the concrete floor was awash with rainwater. What did I care though, it was my birthday!

Joyce wished me a Happy Birthday and then handed me a card that she had drawn herself with crayons.

At hair combing Nurse Mollette put a wave in my hair, before tying it with ribbons. Then prior to breakfast being served, Sister Devereaux called me over to her desk and was smiling.

"Happy Birthday, Forget-Me-Not," she said and then she handed me my cards and presents.

I returned to my place at the breakfast table and I began to open everything.

The presents were from Mam and Dad, aunties and uncles, and also our next door neighbours, and also a small gift from Joyce's mummy and daddy.

I opened my cards and in addition to family and neighbours there was a card signed by Sister Devereaux, Staff Nurse Briggs and Nurse Mollett.

I was joyful as we set off on our morning walk. The rain had stopped and although I would have preferred to be at home with my family I nevertheless felt a belonging. All that day I was made to feel special, both by friends and staff. At teatime I noticed a white square box on Sister's desk, and when we had finished our tea she opened the box and carefully took out a sponge cake, the top of which had fine icing. She added a little candle to the top and lit it, and then picking up the cake and walking over to me and she smiled.

"Make a wish, and then blow."

I closed my eyes and wished for discharge, and then I blew out the candle.

Nurse Mollette cut the cake into as many pieces as possible, and it was shared out between all the girls within my age group. I was sorry that the cake could not share out a little wider, but the modest cake was simply not big enough.

It was the ward concert that evening and it was the turn of one of the boy's wards to put on a show, so we knew the theme would probably be cowboys as usual, since they were the clothes they most often chose from the costumes-trunks.

The audience was settled, the pianist was at her piano.

Then one of the doctors stood up.

"There is a birthday girl in the audience tonight. Would Eleanor Eadie please stand up."

As I rose from my seat the pianist began to play and then everyone sang '*Happy Birthday To You!*' especially for me.

It had truly been a birthday to remember.

Chapter 40.

In the first week of November daylight was in short supply, for we rose and also went to bed in the dark.

Nights in Fortitude Ward were no longer pleasant. Every child scampered into bed as quickly as possible to escape the night winds. Coughing in the mornings, which had always been a hated task, was now dreaded, for there was no way to keep warm whilst leaning over the side of a bed. All of the fortitude girls were complaining, and I thought to myself that they would moan even louder if, like me, they had endured this ritual for more than a year.

Everyone knew I had been in the hospital the longest, and I was quickly pointed out to new patients, giving me a status I would have preferred not to have.

Why was I being kept in when I had put on weight? When I had been admitted every bone in my body had been visible, and my ribs could easily have been counted, but not any more.

Also it was no longer considered necessary to keep my hair shot, and it was starting to grow longer. It was now parted down the middle and tied with two ribbons, and Sister had told me that when it was long enough I could have plaits. So why was I still here? Every time there had been a medical I had been optimistic. Now I knew that I had to be discharged and therefore I would be spared having to spend another January and February sleeping in Fortitude Ward, for those two months were the worst of all.

Last November Christmas spirit had been in the air, for we had been rehearsing '*Silent Night*' in readiness for our visitors' Christmas treat. My days had been happily spent with Christine, and I had found no reason then to think that I would be waiting so long for my turn to go home.

However this November did turn out be different. On the Monday of the second week of November someone accidentally activated the fire extinguisher that stood beside the dining room door.

Unlike modern fire extinguishers this one was large and heavy and stood over four feet high and attached to its top was a length of flexible hose with a nozzle on the end.

Girls had begun to queue outside the dining room for their teatime meal. Joyce, Rosie and I were just about finished with the shoe-cleaning and were looking forward to the hot shower when we heard a loud hissing and when we looked towards the wedged open door, and for a split second, there came from the the corridor a jet of white foam that sprayed about the doorway. The long hose was writhing and it seemed to rear up in the washroom doorway. It shot a fierce jet of past us that went out through a washroom window and with perfect aim entered an open cookhouse window on the other side of the path, such the intensity of it.

We hurried to the door to look out into the corridor to see what was happening and saw the long extinguisher hose thrashing about like an angry snake as the foam escaped under pressure. There was foam on the ceiling and running down the walls and across the floor. Sister Devereaux, Staff Nurse Briggs and many other nurses were quickly on the scene, but their uniforms rapidly became foamy and wet. Nurse Mollett took off her foamed glasses and then accidentally dropped them. We watched as she frantically searched the heaps of foam until she found them again.

Then Maintenance men and cleaners with mops and buckets arrived.

It would all have been such slapstick fun, had we not been acutely aware of the reprisals that would follow.

As for the performance, it was not yet over. Everyone had to bathe - yet again. Staff had to change into clean uniforms and we were all assembled rather late in the dining room as a result.

Sister took her place at her desk with an expression on her face that left us in no doubt how annoyed she was with us.

We all sat mute, waiting for Sister top speak, but she remained silent.

The door opened and Matron entered. She walked over to the desk in her slow and stiff way, as if her shoes were pinching her feet, and then she stood facing us in a most menacing way.

"Will the girl who activated the fire extinguisher please step forward," she said with great precision.

No one moved.

Matron was in her mid fifties, had grey hair and was thick set. She wore a dark blue uniform and a very small white frilly cap. She was, needless to say, a very formidable woman and had a long face with a square jaw and small beady blue eyes that were aiming around the room and scrutinising every girl.

"I Will ask one more time - will the culprit please step forward."

No one moved, and whilst we were all no doubt wishing someone would own up. I could not blame whoever it was for not doing so, for Matron looked so awful as anger contorted her stern features.

She seethed.

"I will not tolerate behaviour of this kind in the hospital," she said. "It is obvious the culprit is not going to come forward, therefore you will all be punished."

Once again her small piercing eyes were surveying. She pinched her lips together, giving her face an even squarer appearance, and then she continued.

"You will all retire at six o' clock each evening for two weeks. No playtimes, no talking in bed. Is that understood?"

"*Yes Matron,*" we all replied together with a kind of agony.

Then she raised a hand.

"The only exception will be Sundays, when you will attend religious instruction as usual."

Her lips pressed together again and then she dropped her bombshell.

"In order to ensure there is no repetition of your atrocious behaviour I shall be giving serious consideration to the cancelling of the next visiting day. Your behaviour from now on will influence my decision. I trust these measures will ensure that you all learn from the error of your ways," she said.

Then Matron turned around and had a quiet word with Sister Devereaux and then she walked with the same pained step to the door. She departed, leaving us all stunned and saddened by her final cruel words.

Then Sister Devereaux addressed us.

"I do not intend to say any more on this subject tonight," she said. "You will shortly be given a hot drink and then you will retire to bed, even it is now," and she glanced at her watch, "only five thirty p.m."

We could not believe it. Was that all Sister had to say? We had been expecting a lecture, but instead she was unusually quiet.

Her hair was still damp and rather flat on the top, for usually it was piled high and springy over her forehead, and always neat. But now there were little tendrils of loose hairs curling around her face.

So reluctantly we began the first of fourteen nights of going to bed early. What a miserable two weeks it was going to be.

The next day at breakfast we steeled ourselves in readiness for the wrath of Sister Devereaux as we sat facing her after breakfast. To our great surprise she once again had little to say. There was not a word of reprimand, except for saying that she felt we owed staff an apology for yesterday's fiasco.

This was all very strange, and not at all in keeping with her normal behaviour following misdemeanours by patients.

During our morning walk the events of the previous day, and Sister's unusual calmness that morning was the topic of conversation.

One girl added to the speculation.

"She will be waiting until teatime before she punished us" she said, "because that is her way when we loose our hankies."

However, upon arriving back at the hospital for our lunch there was no sign of Sister Devereaux or Staff Nurse Briggs deputising. Everyone wanted to know where Sister was, until Staff Nurse Briggs told us Sister was not feeling well and would be absent for the rest of the day.

So that was it. Sister was poorly.

I did not like to think of Sister feeling ill and I hoped she would soon be better and back at her desk. I looked around at the other girls but no one seemed the least bit worried that Sister was missing. Was there only me who really liked her? It was perhaps because I had known her so much longer than the other girls and had come to understand her better than the others did.

During our shoe-cleaning session a group of nurses could be heard talking and the three of us tried hard to hear what they were talking about.

It was hard to hear full sentences but we did manage to hear snippets, such as: "*I could not believe she really walked out!*" and "*She lost her temper and then left - just like that!*" Then: "*No one has ever stood their ground with Matron before!*" Then in the embers of the excitement we heard: "*it is a pity she has lost her job though.*"

Their conversation became inaudible as they walked out of earshot, and we shoe-cleaners sat looking at each other and wondering who the nurses might have been talking about.

Rosie voiced her opinion.

"I am glad someone has upset Matron because she looks so evil. When she gave out the punishment she was actually enjoying it."

I sighed.

"Yes, she looks like an evil old witch," I said.

Joyce felt moved to speak.

"Then I wish she would jump on her broomstick and fly away!" she said.

Pleased that someone had upset Matron we could not wait to pass on the news.

That night we once again went to bed early, and I hoped Sister would feel better and be back at her desk in the morning.

I was downhearted when I discovered that it was Staff Nurse Briggs who was once again in charge. After I had eaten my breakfast I went over to her Sister was feeling any better.

Staff Nurse Briggs replied.

"I do not know."

During our walk that morning we shoe-cleaners related to the rest of the girls what we had overheard the evening before. Everyone was delighted that someone had upset Matron.

One of the older girls had a theory.

"It might have been Sister Devereaux who walked out," she said, "after all she is is not here, is she?"

Another girl answered.

"Let's hope it is Sister, then we can have Staff Nurse Briggs all of the time."

It felt like an ice cold dagger had been plunged into my stomach. Surely Sister Deveraux had not walked out. What if I was to never ever see her again?

I felt I could not face another day in the hospital if Sister was not around. Yet if it were true and Sister was gone then I would even more desperately want to go home, because my days in the hospital would be miserable without her.

I silently repeated a little prayer over and over in my mind that she would return, whilst girls around me were expressing their own wishes that Sister Devereaux should be gone forever.

As a result of this I felt out of sorts during the whole of my morning walk and upon returning to the hospital I took little interest in the school lesson. Even the delicious smell of dinner escaping from the cookhouse failed to cheer me.

When we entered the dining room for our midday meal I felt a surge of joy and relief when I saw Sister Devereaux was seated at her desk. My prayer had been answered and a feeling of happiness and contentment replaced my melancholy. The girls had been mistaken and it was not Sister who had had an argument with Matron and then walked out.

I did not care about the fourteen early nights any more.

I was in high spirits for the rest of the afternoon, and even more at teatime when Sister announced.

"Matron has reviewed her punishment for the fire extinguisher incident. Your early night have been reduced from fourteen to seven. Visiting day will take place as usual."

"*Thank you, Sister,*" we all replied together.

This meant we had only five early nights remaining, and we were all relieved that visiting day had not been cancelled - its being so very important to us.

We never did find out who had activated the fire extinguisher. The culprit never owned up, and if anyone had witnessed the mischief then they also kept it to themselves. The foam had made a mess of the corridor's polished floor, and for weeks afterwards the sound of cleaners could be heard waxing and buffing twice daily.

Chapter 41.

The preparations for Christmas 1948 seemed a replica of Christmas 1947, except that every girl who had attended the previous festivities had gone home to enjoy Christmas with their families once again.

We were busy in the schoolroom making paper chains and once again children were selected from all four sections, there being twelve wards in the hospital in total.

As regards The Christmas Nativity Play. I was chosen to take part and so was Joyce, plus two other girls from Sister Devereaux's section.

All four of us would be angels.

Just as the previous year the general public were admitted for a fee to watch us perform. Photographs were once again taken, and this year my parents could afford to buy a print of the photograph, which I have to this day.

Sister again fooled everyone on Christmas Day, just as before, by saying there was school.

I enjoyed all of the festivities, even though the element of surprise in many quarters was missing - or at least I thought it was, for I was wrong.

Something happened on Christmas Day that no one could possibly have foreseen.

We all went to bed on Christmas Eve absolutely tingling with excitement, and were awake long before the night nurse came around with the coughing bowls. We eagerly fetched our presents out from under our beds. There was such ecstasy and chatter as excited children were opening their presents - the wrappings being torn off and many small miracles being revealed. My present from Mam and Dad was a little cardboard dolls' house with cotton wool on the roof to make it look as if it had been snowing. Inside there were tiny wooden chairs, a table and a bed, plus a dolly.

The noise of children was deafening, but as loud as it was one particular child's cry rose high above the din.

It was a scream, so high pitched and intense that it was almost sinister in quality - as if the girl had come face to face with a demonic monster.

Everyone in the ward gradually stopped talking as the screaming continued.

The girl's bed was on the back row nearest the corridor and third and third on from the dining room wall. I was on the middle row and third left from Patience Ward, so when I turned around to look at her I had a full view.

Her name was Shirley Hunter, a seven year old girl with dark brown hair and brown eyes. She was sat up in bed with tears streaming down her face and her mouth wide open. Her lips and features were crumpled with emotion. I feared she was choking between the screams, for she had such difficulty getting her breath.

Sister Kilshaw and the night nurse came running, but there was nothing they could do to comfort Shirley, for it soon became apparent that Santa Claus had forgotten her.

There was not a single present under her bed.

There was absolutely nothing at all.

Our joy turned to anguish, for I had never seen such a heart-rending sight in my life before.

The harsh truth was that through accident or design she had received no presents, even from her family and the absence had been overlooked in the hurry and distractions of the festive season.

In a mood that approaching despair we each decided to give Shirley one of our presents. Each of us in turn walked over to Shirley's bed and placed a gift on it for her counterpane.

Shirley, being in shock, could not respond and sat there screaming and utterly heartbroken.

Our individual donations made little difference because The Spirit of Christmas himself had not delivered them to her and our making a allowance with our own presents was far from being the same thing.

The awfulness of seeing Shirley so upset had subdued us all.

Finally the nurse took Shirley in her arms and took her out of the ward, and we could hear those pitiful screams grow fainter as she was carried away.

All the gifts we had given her lay untouched on her bed.

This had to be the worst Christmas morning I had ever had and, indeed, was ever likely to have again. Every other patient was deeply affected by the incident and a sorrowful hush hung over the ward.

We all spoke in private about poor little Shirley and were voiced our fears of what it must be like to be unloved and forgotten.

The only thing we could do was to reserve all kindness for Shirley, whilst we all felt the agony and trustration of knowing there was nothing we could do.

We did not see Shirley until we were in the concert room for our Christmas Dinner, when Sister Devereaux led her to her place at the table.

Shirley was not crying any more, but her eyes were downcast.

We all began trying to make her feel she was the most important little girl at the dinner table as we passed her the contents from our Christmas crackers.

Then Santa came on stage and was calling out the names of children. When Shirley's name was called she refused to move. Olga, the eldest girl at the table, stood up and took Shirley's hand but Shirley refused to leave her seat. Then Sister Devereaux walked over and Shirley offered no resistance to Sister and it was Sister who led Shirley up onto the stage to receive her present, and we all wondered what excuse there could possibly be for Santa not remembering her.

The following morning Shirley was in better spirits and to everyone's relief she began to play with the gifts we had given her. Each and every one of us was extremely attentive to her needs and made sure she was at the centre of all our activities.

We had all found it impossible to conceive of how a little girl so far from home could be completely ignored by her community at home on such an occasion. It made us all acutely aware of just how privileged we were to be loved and cherished by our families and their friends and neighbours.

After the Christmas holiday, when all the shops were again open, Sister came in one morning with a box wrapped in gift paper and placed it on her desk. After breakfast she picked up the box and walked over to Shirley.

Crouching down beside Shirley, Sister smiled.

"This is a present for a very special little girl." she said.

Shirley opened the present eagerly and inside was a large spinning-top that was decorated with bright characters. On the top was a screw-plunger, which when pressed made the top spin and hum.

Shirley was full of smiles, and even Joyce, who disliked Sister more than most of the other girls, had to admit that this was a thoughtful thing to do for the girl that Christmas had forgotten.

Chapter 42.

It was now the first week in January 1949 and it was the day before the medicals. I had been in the hospital since October 1947, much longer than any other patient, and I felt sure that I would be discharged this time. Sister had allowed my hair hair to grow even longer and it was long enough to tie back in two bunches. Soon I would be able to have the long-awaited plaits, and this for me was an indication that I getting better.

I did not want to spend another winter in the hospital, for it was bitterly cold again in those long dark nights. I had remembered the winter of 1947-1948 all too well. Fortitude Ward offered little protection from the elements. To have to leave the warmth of the dining room and enter Fortitude Ward each evening was unpleasant in the extreme. No person in their right mind would spend the cruel months of January and February sleeping in an open shelter in their back garden, and yet that was what we were doing. True, we had three solid walls, but the wind raced through and the rain lashed through the wire-netting as if we had no protection at all. The beds were metal and to accidentally place one's hand on the bed head resulted in a sudden reflex action as if one had been burned.

I thought back to the previous year and the morning coughing in freezing temperatures and how we all had chilblains on our feet while some had them on their hands. How chapped and sore my lips had become, cracking and bleeding if I smiled too broadly. The current contingent of patients in Fortitude Ward did not know what was in store for them, but I felt certain that I would not be one of that winter's victims. I would soon be home with my family and I would be warm and snug in my own bed.

The next morning I rose with a smile on my face and I could not wait for the medicals to begin. Everyone was hopeful of going home. Olga decided I was definitely leaving.

"You will be discharged, " she said, "because you have been here such a long time."

Joyce who was listening decided to speak.

"I hope I will be going home too, Eleanor," she said. "I could not face life in this hospital without you as my friend."

I tried to reassure her.

"You'll soon make another friend," I said. "I felt exactly the same and then you came along."

My words failed to console her.

"Perhaps we shall both be discharged together," I said.with a smile.

I waited with the others for a medical examination and when my name was called I rubbed my hands and cheeks to try to make them look rosy and healthy. I walked with as much confidence as I could muster.

In the examination room I was weighed, and yet again I had put on weight. My height was checked, and I found I had grown a little taller. I answered the doctor's questions without faltering, and when they asked me to breathe deeply I could not hear any wheezing at all.

I came out of the consulting room walking on air.

I was now absolutely certain that I would be going home.

I asked Joyce how she had got on and she answered as if to mirror my confidence.

"I have gained a little weight and I am very hopeful," she said.

For the next week nothing could deflate my high mood. I was sure that when Sister read out the names of the girls who were going home then my name would be one of them.

I wondered if my mam and dad had been informed yet. Perhaps they were already celebrating. I found myself checking Mam's letters just in case she had remembered the code of a year ago, but I decided she must have forgotten, for all letters ended with '*Mam and Dad.*'

Oh what a long ten days that was. I found it difficult to sleep at night time, for all I could only think about my going home. The days dragged on at a snail's pace but eventually the day arrived when the names of the girls who were going home was to be read out.

When we had all finished our breakfasts, Sister called for silence and began reading the names of the girls who had been discharged.

As I listened I heard the names of girls who had been in the hospital less than half the time than I had been here.

Then all of a sudden I could not believe it. She had not read out any names beginning with 'E.'

Perhaps Sister was having a little joke, therefore still with half a smile on my face I waited for my name to be called out after the end.

However Sister folded the sheet of paper, saying:

"That completes the list of the girls who have been discharged."

I sat there completely stunned.

It was not a joke after all. I really had not been discharged.

Then I felt like I was dreaming, and that I was going to wake up and find none of this was true. It could not be true! Why would they keep me here when anyone could see how healthy I was?

Joyce's name had not been included either, and she turned to me.

"I am so sorry," she said.

I turned on her like a wild cat.

"You are *lying*!" I said. "You are pleased I am not going home!"

Then rising from my seat I ran out of the dining room and into the washroom where I buried my face in the roller - towel and I cried like I had never cried before.

"Why was I not going home?

The washroom door opened and Nurse Mollett entered. She knelt and took me in her arms and hugged me closely to her.

She let me cry, holding me until all my tears were spent.

Then she addressed my awful disappointment.

"The doctor obviously does not consider you completely well," she said. "And he is a clever man who knows his job."

"But I am being punished," I said. "I am being kept prisoner and I will never be going home."

"That is silly talk, Eleanor," she said. "Do you really think the doctor would keep you here if it was not absolutely necessary."

She waited until I nodded.

"So don't you start getting thoughts like that again," she said. "So you give me a big hug and a kiss,"

I kissed her and wet her face with my abundant tears.

Then Nurse Mollett had me stand up straight.

"I am going to tell you a secret and it is good news. I am getting married soon," she said, "but I would be even happier if you to make me a special card to wish me and Derek well on our wedding day, and what is more I will keep that card forever," she said.

"I will make you a card," I said whilst dabbing at my face.

Nurse Mollett led me out of the washroom and back into the dining room and was just about to say something further when Sister called Nurse Mollett over to her desk. So I rejoined Joyce, who upon seeing I had been crying was very attentive, forgetting all about the harsh words I had said.

The next medicals would be in April, so, yet again, I was going to have to endure another winter in Fortitude Ward. I felt depressed and my head was aching from crying. I placed my hands upon the table and resting my chin in my palms I closed my eyes whilst my head throbbed and my heart ached with misery.

Some time later I slowly opened my eyes and realised that I had been asleep. I raised my head and stretched my arms in an attempt to relieve them of stiffness. I saw around me that girls were sat around in groups talking but that Joyce remained seated at the side of me.

"You slept through Sister's talks to the girls who are not being discharged," she said before sending me a resentful look, "but you did not miss much," as if it had been a further torment.

She shrugged her shoulders,

"I wanted to be talked to by Nurse Mollett," then she pulled a face, "but I got frosty Sister Devereaux instead, which was really no help at all."

I did not know exactly why she disliked Sister Devereaux so much, because Sister was nice once you got to know and understand her.

I was about to explain this to her when Joyce gave me a withering look.

"I will NEVER like her, ever!"

I went to the washroom to wash my face and when I looked at myself in the mirror I looked awful. My eyes were swollen from crying and I had pressure marks on one cheek from where my face had been lying on my hands.

I returned to the dining room long after the midday meal was served.

After my meal Sister said she wished to talk to me.

The other girls went for their thirty minutes rest on their beds, where they should be 'cocooned' in blankets by the nurses so as to fend off the cold.

"Sit beside me, Eleanor," Sister Devereaux said.

Then when I was settled she spoke.

"You are disappointed because you have not been discharged. However, do you know why? Tell me."

"Because of the doctor," Sister," I said.

"Answer my question. Why were you not discharged?" she asked.

"Because he says I am still not better," I replied.

She placed her fingers under my chin and forced me to look up into her eyes.

222

"I want an honest answer this time. For what reason were you not discharged?"

I once again tried to lower my gaze but her hand remained and I was forced to look at her.

"Because they want to keep me in here," I said with anguish, "even though I am better now."

"Who are '*they*,' Eleanor?" she asked.

"The doctors, Sister," I explained. "I am not thin any more and I hardly cough now and I have put on weight and look at me I am taller now," I said as proof.

Then I felt the gloominess return.

"But still they will not let me go home, Sister, I feel like a prisoner here."

"Eleanor, you are not a prisoner here," Sister said before studying me.

"The reason the doctor has not discharged you is purely and simply because he feels you are not quite fit enough to go home."

She paused and studied my face until I was watching her closely.

"In this hospital you are monitored every single day by experts in the field, and given the appropriate dose of medication. Do you believe you would receive this standard of medical care if you were allowed to go home prematurely?

I studied for a moment.

"My mam and dad love me very much," I said.

"You are not listening to what I am saying, Eleanor. Love does not come into it. I am referring to expert medical care. Well?"

"No. Sister," I said, "I don't suppose I would," I replied meekly.

"There is no 'suppose' about it! You would see your family doctor at best once a week, perhaps even less. Am I making myself clear?"

"Yes, Sister."

"I want you to bear this in mind and refrain from harbouring dark thoughts. Instead I want you to be grateful for all the effort that is being put into restoring you to health."

The she watched me.

"At times I think this gratitude is lacking."

Her final words hurt me.

Could she not see how much I appreciated her? Did she not understand how I admired and almost worshipped her? She was my idol and the most vital part of my life in the hospital.

I felt a desperate need to tell her how much I valued her efforts. With any other person I would have shown it with hugging and kissing, but with Sister this was out of the question. I was not able to find words to express my feelings and my tears of frustration began to form in my eyes.

Then she noticed my tears.

"*Now* what is the matter?"

I felt a surge of temper.

"You are wrong, Sister," I said suddenly. "I am grateful to you every single day," I said. "But you do not know that because there is never a way to tell you!"

I paused to wipe away my tears while she waited and so I continued.

"For me you are the most important person in the hospital. I am so miserable when you are not here."

Then to make absolutely sure that she knew how I felt I added:

"I love you, Sister," I said.

I had voiced the feelings that I had been hiding for so long.

Sister watched me.

"Where is your handkerchief, Eleanor? Dry your eyes."

I fumbled in my pocket, found my hankie and dried my eyes and blew my nose, whilst she turned to sit forward behind her desk and gazed absent-mindedly at it.

"This is a hospital, Eleanor, and the emotions you are experiencing are not uncommon when one is separated from loved ones, as you have been for such an inordinate length of time. Whilst I appreciate the sentiments you have expressed you will nevertheless upon discharge go home and never see me again. I shall be quickly forgotten once you are reunited with your family, It is very important that you appreciate this. I see so many girls come and go and my reward is the knowledge is that I have contributed to them being able to live full and healthy lives. I ask for nothing more than this."

Reaching for my hand, she said:

"You are correct in your assumption that you are getting better, and I am certain your discharge is not very far away. In the meantime try to make the time you have in the hospital as happy as possible."

She watched me again.

"Come on, smile for me Forget-Me-Not."

I tried to smile and she smiled back and then she dismissed me.

I rejoined the rest of the girls who were now rising from their beds and we all made our way to the schoolroom for the afternoon's hour of tuition.

I remembered Sister's words.

'Upon discharge you will go home and never see me again.'

I had been so obsessed with thoughts of going home that it had not once occurred to me that when I left the hospital I would never see Sister regularly again. The bond that I had nurtured with Sister Devereaux was so strong that I could not contemplate living my life without her being a part of it. Although I saw my mam for one hour every six weeks I was otherwise near constantly in Sister Devereaux's presence.

She was wrong. I would never forget her and I knew that she would be etched in my memory for the rest of my life.

Following school we went on our afternoon walk, which, surprisingly, I enjoyed. It was along the promenade The winter sun, now low in the sky and afforded very little heat but was making the frosted ground sparkle like diamonds. I noticed a spider's web bejewelled with frost beneath a sign that read: '*No Bathing.*' Then when I looked out across the cold grey waters of the Dee I thought how inappropriate the sign was was on a cold January afternoon.

A solitary couple were feeding the marine birds a little further along the promenade, throwing bread down onto the water of the high tide where the gulls were flocking. We stood watching the antics the birds. They competed with each other for every single crumb. If a bird artfully snatched a piece of bread it would flap its wings furiously, raising itself out of the water in a little victory display.

I was feeling in a much better mood for my thoughts had turned to making a very special card for Nurse Mollett.

Joyce, who also liked Mollett had said she would make one too.

Walking along together we were discussing our designs and I explained my card first.

"I have decided on a card with a bride and groom on the front, then on the inside there will be a big red heart," I said.

My unhappiness at not being discharged had vanished and I no longer considered spending a further three months in the hospital a daunting prospect. The reason was that for those months would be spent with Sister Devereaux and I would relish every moment before finally saying goodbye to her for ever.

Chapter 43.

One evening around a week later I was lying in my bed after talking time was over and the lights had been turned off. A cold January wind was blowing through the wire netting and across our faces, along with the odd spot of rain. The nurses had tucked all of us in tightly and our bodies were warm and snug and I was relaxed and slowly drifting into slumber.

I then became aware of Sister Kilshaw' usual routine, walking as silently as a shadow up and down the ward to make sure all was well. However instead of her leaving she walked over to my bed and began peering at me over the top of her spectacles, checking if I was asleep.

I looked blearily at her.

"Goodnight, Sister Kilshaw."

Expecting her to reply with her usual '*God Bless*,' I was surprised to find she did not.

"Ah, you are awake, that is g-good," she said. "I want you to put on your dressing-g-gown and slippers and come with me, Eleanor."

I sleepily obeyed, slipping my hand into hers and walking beside her as the cobwebs of sleep were still clouding my thoughts. I rubbed at my eyes with my free hand, taking little notice of where she was taking me. Then I when became more alert I realised I was in an unfamiliar room.

It was something like a sitting room. A fire was burning merrily in a grate in a fireplace and while positioned to face it were four upholstered armchairs. I was shown to one and I found it to be rather worn but comfortable.

A radio was stood on a table in a corner whilst in another corner there was a kitchen sink and beside it a kitchen cabinet on which there was set a gas ring and a kettle and a tea caddy while some white earthenware cups and saucers were there also.

Behind me and in the centre of the room I had seen a small table on which two cups of steaming tea had been placed and also an ashtray containing numerous cigarette stubs.

It was then that from the doorway there entered a woman who came to stand on the faded hearthrug before the fire.

Facing me was a fair-haired blue-eyed woman with short cropped hair who was wearing colourful clothes. Her dress was low cut and showed a gold-coloured necklace, while on her wrist was a matching bracelet. Her earrings had tiny golden fishes dangling on them that the light caught as she turned her head. She wore high-heeled shoes and seemed to be waiting for me to speak.

Next she stepped away to place her lit cigarette in the ashtray and when she returned and then opened her arms towards me, expecting me to embrace her.

I could not imagine who she was, so I sat stock still and silent.

It was then that I recognised her.

It was Nurse Owens.

It was the voice that I recognised when she spoke,

"Hello, Eleanor," she said in her soft lilting Welsh tones.

I knew her so well, yet here there was undoubtedly a stranger. Gone were the shoulder-lengths locks, replaced by a trendy hairstyle that completely changed her appearance. She was wearing heavy make-up including startlingly bright red lipstick, while her clothes were fashionable and striking.

I stared in disbelief, for she was barely recognisable. Her severe hairstyle had hardened her features and her heavy use of cosmetics masked the simple youthful charm that I had once so admired.

She stepped closer and knelt down began talking to me, telling me about the job she was now doing.

"But although I am very happy there, Eleanor," she said, "I do miss all the children of this hospital."

I spoke in an especially polite way when I tanswering all of her questions, but I would not kiss her or put my arms around her because she was not Nurse Owens any more. She was not the Nurse Owens I had known and loved. She seemed a part of another world. As we said goodbye she gave me a kiss on my cheek and the smell of her heavy perfume surrounded me.

Sister Kilshaw led me from the room and back to my warm bed where I lay thinking about what had happened. At first I wondered why I had been singled out, and then it occurred to me that most of the girls whom she had known had been discharged.

I then began to feel that I ought to have embraced her, for I had seen her disappointment when I did not leave my chair and run into her arms.

If only she could have looked the same as I had remembered her, dressed in her nurse's uniform, her face without make-up and her long golden hair pinned under her cap. Then I would have run to her and showered her with kisses.

She had changed, from a pretty young girl into a grown-up stylish woman. Her face masked, her youthful ways replaced by the perfumes and trappings of the age.

Nurse Owens had been the star in my sky, an image of the wondrous beauty and gentleness that I had craved for myself,and I had found o imperfections in her. That image had now been shattered, along with an era of my young life, for that Nurse Owens no longer existed.

The idol I had hero-worshipped had fled.

Chapter 44.

I quickly forgot about Nurse Owens when the next day I discovered there was a change to the routine, a routine that I was accustomed to being utterly unchangeable.

After breakfast, Sister made an announcement.

"Some visitors from a charity are to address us all in the concert hall. Your morning walk is cancelled and instead every child in the hospital who is well enough to listen will attend You shall wear your Sunday clothes and you are to be on your best behaviour."

This was something I had never known happen before. I decided these people must be very important indeed if we all had to make such an effort. I was glad of the abandoned walk because snowflakes were in the air about the grounds. At least we would be dry and warm in the concert hall.

In the concert hall Matron, with her usual stiff gait, made her way up the stage steps with difficulty and walked up to an old fashioned brown microphone. Then after a few words she introduced the visitors from the charity and asked us all to warmly welcome them. Then after the applause three men and three women in navy blue uniforms with gold trim walked onto the stage and each visitor said a few words.

Joyce and I, at least, did not understand what they were talking about and I was beginning to wish they would say what they had to say and go, whilst I noticed lots of children were beginning to fidget.

At last, after what seemed an eternity, the speeches were over and we all applauded once again, even though I at least had no notion of what they had said.

The visitors then left the stage, and after five minutes we were all given permission to leave the concert room in an orderly manner.

First were the children in wheelchairs and then the rest of us, though only one row at a time, beginning with the back row. There was the sound of shuffling as the procession grew.

Eventually it came to our turn and as we walked through the door we saw the six uniformed visitors were stood there handing out parcels that they were fetching from large boxes. Every child was being given a parcel so that suddenly our boredom turned into excitement.

What were they giving us?

One of the men spoke to me.

"And what is your name?" he asked.

"Eleanor," I said politely.

"Well I do hope you will soon be better soon, Eleanor, and that you will be able to go home soon," he said kindly.

We all walked back down the long corridor clutching our parcels, each of us curious as to what they contained.

Some girls shook them to see if the contents rattled.

I usually enjoyed the long routes through the hospital but today the corridor seemed never ending, and I wanted to run to shorten the walk, but running was strictly forbidden.

We at last reached the dining room and Sister Devereaux gave us permission to open our parcels.

Everyone was frantically tearing at the brown paper to discover the contents.

I found to my delight that my parcel contained half a dozen toys. None of them were new and they had obviously been donated to a good cause. I cannot remember everything that was in my parcel but I do recall a wooden jigsaw with a picture of Princesses Elizabeth and Margeret. They were shown playing with a doll's house that had been given to them by the people of Wales. They were only small children in the photograph and in my time they had grown up - and in fact Princess Elizabeth was now married, yet to me the jigsaw was a treasure.

The joy in the dining room was indescribable. I did feel guilty that I had not paid more attention to what had been said during the speeches. I felt an immense gratitude to all those who had donated the toys, for such surprises as these brought great comfort to children who were far from home

Chapter 45.

On February 1st 1949 clothes rationing ended in Britain.

All of the nurses celebrated.

They were constantly chatting about the wave of change infashionthat was called 'The New Look," for Christian Dior's revolution in women's style would finally be available in the shops, and even the young nurses would be able to afford them.

Every evening after my attention was firmly focussed on the nurses going off duty in their latest purchases while the boys hung around the gates hoping to catch their attentions.

Another week had passed almost uneventfully I we were again to fall victim to the wintry February weather. Once again I had chilblains on my feet and on my lips. I was given cream to put on my lips as often as possible but it did not seem to help. We walked in practically all weathers, no matter how cold or wet. The only weather condition that kept us indoors was fog, for it was not considered in our best interest to be breathing in the pollutants trapped in the mist.

Joyce complained bitterly, for she also had chilblains on her hands and feet, though she did not have sore lips like me. However, unlike the winter of 1947 to 1948 I was not unhappy.

Last winter I had disliked Sister Devereaux, but this winter I adored her, and that made such a difference to my life and how I coped with the adversities of the cold dark wintry days and nights.

Nurse Mollett had now married her Derek, and we had each made her a congratulations card, and even the little five year olds had made the effort, for Nurse Mollett was very well liked. She was quite emotional when she looked at all the cards that we had taken such pains to make for her and she promised that she would keep them all forever. We were all so pleased to see her so happy. Our joy was short-lived however, for she would soon be leaving the hospital due to her husband finding a better job in another part of the country.

Everyone felt the loss when they heard the news.

The days passed and all too soon it was the second Friday in the month of February, which was Nurse Mollett's last day in the hospital.

We had all finished our midday meal but instead of spending thirty minutes lying on our beds Sister told us to remain seated as Nurse Mollett was to be presented with a leaving present and it had been decided that we could watch the presentation.

In the dining room were Sister Devereaux, Staff Nurse Briggs and all the nurses on duty, some of whom worked in other sections of the hospital. I had never seen the dining room so full of people before. Nurses were sitting wherever they could and those who could not find a seat stood by the piano waiting for it all to begin. We children were all sat excitedly because we had never seen a leaving presentation before.

One particular nurse was missing however and that was Nurse Mollett herself.

As if reading my mind a nurse asked where Nurse Mollett actually was.

Sister smiled wryly.

"I have sent her out of the way with a false errand to fetch something that is not there, but she will be with us shortly," she explained.

We all sat waiting.

My thoughts went back to my first day in this dining room when I had sat staring at the glass doorknob on the dining room door. This time I found myself doing the same thing, only this time watching for Nurse Mollett. Nurse Mollet had been my first real acquaintance on the day I arrived. In her thick spectacles and with her fears almost as pronounced as my own we had forged, in my mind at least, an unlikely alliance

The door opened and Nurse Mollett walked in, looking exasperated after her difficulties.

"Sister I could not find any of the..." and then she stopped.

She put her hands up to her face with embarrassment and then spun around and smiled happily at everyone.

Sister Devereaux stepped forward and addressed Nurse Mollett and all of us.

"Well, Nurse Mollett, today sadly you are leaving. You have been with us for over two years, and I know that everyone present, and those that cannot be here today, will know how sorry we are to see you go. You have been very popular and a most valued member of staff."

Then Sister turned to fetch something from her desk.

"We have all appreciated your high standard of work and valued your friendship, and so as a token of our respect and gratitude we have had a collection, to which all of your friends and colleagues have given generously, I might add. It is therefore my pleasure, on behalf of everyone here, to present you with a parting gift."

Sister handed a gift-wrapped parcel to Nurse Mollett before saying:

"I wish you and your husband every happiness in your future life together."

Sister then kissed Nurse Mollett and gave her a warm hug, and then everyone in the room clapped their hands.

Nurse Mollett opened the parcel and revealed that the gift was a porcelain figurine of an Edwardian lady.

Nurse Mollett took a handkerchief from her pocket, took off her spectacles and wiped her eyes. Then replacing her glasses she said:

"Well first of all let me say," and she paused again and and looked around, "That I never expected anything like this. My sincere thanks to everyone who put money towards this very beautiful gift."

Then she smiled again.

"I appreciate it so very much."

Everyone clapped their hands as Nurse Mollett walked up to Sister and gave her a kiss and then she kissed Staff Nurse Briggs too.

Then she turned to us children and said:

"I want to thank each and every one of you girls for the wonderful cards you havemade," she said with high emotion. "I shall keep them always and I shall miss you all."

We all clapped again while some of us, including myself, were fighting off tears.

Nurses were all too soon returning to their duties while we would shortly be heading for the schoolroom.

How quickly the routines returned, and how soon we were swept back into our normal habits.

I had watched Sister hug and kiss Nurse Mollett and for a moment I yearned for that. Sister Devereaux was ordinarily so strictly professional with staff and patients and would never hug and kiss me like that. A fierce envy had engulfed me. I had been away from home for so long, and wished for its merest trace wherever I could find it.

Chapter 46.

February passed without note just as the usual daily routine of walking, eating and sleeping in the dark wintry weather was a monotonous one. I no longer had a favourite nurse since Nurse Mollett had left. The nurses were all of them friendly and caring, but I did not warm to any one in particular. Staff Nurse Briggs was nice enough in her way, but my little world revolved around Sister, who like me was a master of routines herself.

March arrived, and although the weather was still wintry at least the days were lengthening and, most important of all, next month there were medicals.

Sister had told me I was almost well enough to go home, so there was a strong possibility that I would be discharged this time. Still uppermost in my mind was the fact that when I walked out of the hospital I would never see Sister Devereaux again. This thought was on my mind day and night, and I was torn between joining my family again and my need for Sister to remain a part of my world Like a boat on a turbulent sea I found my future uncertain without my lighthouse at the edge of the world, without my resolute guardian.

I got a surprise during the first week in March, for after we had finished our midday meal Matron walked into the room. She stood in front of Sister's desk, put on her reading glasses and glanced at a sheet paper in her hand.

"I want the following girls to step forward please," she said.

Barbara Jones.
Maureen Lowles.
Eleanor Eadie.
Glenda Wood.

We left our benches and stepped forward, wondering what we had done wrong.

Matron then had a quiet word with Sister and then left the room.

236

The remainder of the girls were then sent from the dining room for their thirty minutes lying down on their beds.

When the room was quiet, Sister smiled and said:

"The local theatre has kindly donated some tickets to the hospital for some of the children to see a show. There are only twelve tickets, so Matron has had the difficult task of selecting the recipients from the four sections of the hospital. In this section," she said, "you are the lucky ones."

Relief flooded through us all as we realised the matter at hand was not as dreadful as we thought. Instead we were to be given a treat.

She continued.

"You are to change into your Sunday clothes and return to the dining room," she said.

I was so excited. To go to a theatre in the outside world was like a dream come true. I could not quite believe it. I wished Joyce had been selected too, for I did not know the other girls on the list very well.

I had never changed clothes so quickly. In double-quick time we returned to the dining room, where we next put on winter coats, then the nurse brushed them down to make sure we looked smart.

Sister then gave us a lecture about behaving ourselves, which was the least we expected.

Then when we were ready we walked out through the back door of the hospital where four more girls and eight boys were assembled.

The theatre was within walking distance, so we took partners in a crocodile arranged as two by two.

The nurses suggested that we should split up and walk in partners of boy and girl, but the boys refused to walk with girls, while we girls were definitely not going to walk with boys. In the end the nurses scrapped this idea and we set off as we were.

I had passed this little theatre many times on our walks but I never thought that I would be walking through its doors. It was lovely and warm in the theatre when we were ushered to seating six rows from the stage.

The great curtains were red with golden tassels along their bottom edges while the footlights were giving them a rich ruby glow. There was an audience made up of children with their parents or guardians and I noticed that they were all looking at programmes. We wanted a programme too, but the nurses explained that they did not have any money.

Musicians then entered the orchestra pit and when they were ready the conductor steeped onto his podium and bowed to the audience.

We all applauded eagerly.

Then the band played a tune, the curtains opened, and the show began.

There were dancers, acrobats and singers, but the star of the show was a magician. We watched in awe as he performed tricks that were beyond our abilities to explain. He made things of many sizes and shapes disappear and reappear, and there were many '*Oooohs*' and '*Aaaahs*' from the audience as he did so.,We were spellbound by his magic.

The magician's assistant then came down into the audience to choose some people to help him. Our Glenda Wood was one of those chosen.

How I wished it had been me!

I nevertheless enjoyed watching while Glenda assisted him with an illusion.

When the show was over the entire cast took their bows and we applauded enthusiastically, and when the magician took his bow we all of us stood up and cheered madly.

What a wonderful afternoon it had been! We came out of the theatre so happy.

As we assembled into a crocodile no one cared who walked with who and I found myself walking with a boy for a partner.

The boy's name was Alan, he was twelve years old and we talked and talked about the show. I found him to be really nice and not at all like the boys I had known in my village back home.

I hardly noticed the walk back, we were enjoying ourselves so much.

I was sorry to say goodbye to Alan. He said he would look out for me at the next ward concert and I promised I would look out for him too.

The other girls in Fortitude Ward were green with envy when we arrived back and we told them about our treat. There was speculation on why we four had been chosen.

Joyce was really pleased to see me back in the hospital.

"My day was terrible," she said, " I was so alone without you."

Then at the next ward concert Alan and I sat together. We became a feature of every ward concert after until other girls would tease me.

"You have a boyfriend!" they would call out.

Whether or not in a hospital where boys and girls were segregated there could be any such thing as boyfriends and girlfriends did not stop the rumours. I was happy to talk to Alan and he to me, and for my part I was amazed that I could, for before coming to the hospital I had rarely spoken at all.

Chapter 47.

Once again I watched winter disappear whilst spring spread her greenness everywhere. The grounds seemed carpeted with spring flowers and even the air in Fortitude Ward seemed fragrant.

Easter was approaching, so that one of our lessons in the schoolroom was calligraphy, when we were to demonstrate what we had learned by producing an Easter Card to send home to our parents. I chose green and red ink and then with my fullest concentration I marked the letters and wished my parents and my sister a 'Happy Easter.

Once again there was the ordeal of another medical.

Prior to my previous medicals I had gone to extraordinary lengths to try to appear fit and well. This time I did not bother, because I was not sure what I truly wanted. I might be discharged or might spend another three months with Sister Devereaux. My emotions were in flux, for though I wanted to go home, and I really did. I wanted my life to include time with Sister.

A week later Sister called for our attention, saying:

"I am pleased to announce that the following patients have been discharged."

The fourth name on the list was mine.

I could not believe it!

I had finally been discharged and the news caused a wondrous feeling to engulf me.

I felt like I was dreaming.

Would I really be seeing my home again?

Would I be seeing my little Sister and my cat, Kitty? My sweet little Kitty - I had missed him too, although I doubted he would remember me after such a long time.

Then Joyce's reaction dampened my enthusiasm.

I had been so happy that I had monetarily forgotten about Joyce, and when I finally looked at her I was shocked to see she was trembling and with tears pouring down her face.

Her words when they came were almost grief-stricken.

"How can I cope," she asked me whilst she tried to put on brave face for my benefit.

Sister Devereaux came over.

"Congratulations," she said and smiled. "I will speak to you later."

Then she took poor stricken Joyce by the hand and led her over to her desk, where Joyce was seated and where Sister began talking earnestly to her.

Seeing Joyce's reaction had damaged my happiness. I felt certain that should find another friend after I had gone home, but I knew there was no way that I could convince her of this.

I looked at Sister talking to Joyce. I could not hear what Sister was saying but I knew she would be finding just the right words to say as she always did. Then of course I too was going to miss Sister talking to me in much the same way?

Sister was smiling at Joyce and I knew at that moment that it was how I was going to remember her forever.forever.

Next I knew that I would have to say goodbye to her.

Did I want to leave Sister or did I want to go home?

The answer was that I wanted both, which of course I could not have.

How could I walk away from someone who had entered my silence and reached me?

Then later and despite Sister having talked to Joyce, Joyce was still upset.

"We have one last week together," I said, "because arrangements have to be made."

Over the following days the girls who had been discharged began to go home. I was the very last girl to leave in Sister's section and Joyce and I spent the time totally wrapped in each each other's attentions.

Joyce never left my side for minute.

Two days before I left the hospital she coughed up blood during morning coughing and spitting. The following day the same thing happened and I became very worried.

My thoughts inevitably returned to what had happened to Christine.

On the morning of the April 22nd 1949 I received the clothes my parents had sent in advance. However my parents had misjudged how much I had grown. I was much taller and broader now and the buttons down the back of my satin dress would not fasten, despite the efforts of the nurses. The nurses then resigned to fasten the topmost button and leave things at that. The coat was much the same, the sleeves being bizarrely short while the coat itself was not anywhere near long enough. It was as if the spirit of Alice, so evident when I had arrived, had returned to share her perplexities with me.

I lost count of how many times I said farewell to the girls, however I was also aware that I was saying goodbye whilst envy shone in their eyes.

The hardest goodbye of all was my goodbye to Joyce, who looked so downcast.

We hugged each other. We promised we would write and that we would never forget the deep friendship we had shared. We were both crying as I walked out of the dining room for the last time.

I said goodbye to all of the nurses, but when I looked for Sister Devereaux I could not see her.

Where was she?

I stared about as panic rose within me.

Nurse Wickens came to my side.

"Where is Sister?" I asked desperately.

"You will definitely be seeing her," she assured me and with that she led me through the many fire doors and down the corridor and finally to reception, the room where everything here had begun for me.

It looked exactly the same as the day I had entered, including the oil painting of the dour woman. However her gaze seemed offset by the presence of a large group of children and staff. There were also some men seated in chairs, each with a raincoat folded over his arm and fedora hats set neatly on them, and who were our escorts.

Matron and Sister Devereaux had all the while followed us in, and I felt such relief and gratitude that Sister had not forgotten about me.

Matron wished all of the girls a stiff '*Goodbye*.'

Then turning to me she addressed me firmly.

"You have the dubious honour, young lady, of having had the second longest stay in Fortitude Ward that I can remember."

She then informed the escorts that all of the patients being discharged were ready, and with that she turned stiffly and left.

I looked up at Sister Devereaux who was smiling down at me.

The kneeling she placed her arms around me tightly in a loving embrace and then kissed me on the forehead.

I put my arms around her too and hugged her back, burying my face in her starched white apron. It was something I had longed to do and it was fitting that now my wish had been finally granted.

"My task is complete," she said. "Hopefully you will lead a full and happy life."

Then she watched me as keenly as she had ever done.

"However, you have been restored to health at the expense of your education, Eleanor. I want you to regain the ground you have lost. I know you are capable of doing this."

Then she waited.

"Do this for me, Eleanor. Promise?"

She waited.

"Promise?" she asked again.

"Yes, Sister," I said respectfully, "I will do my best."

She embraced me again.

"Goodbye, Forget-Me-Not."

Chapter 48.

I was found by my escort and I joined the group of boys and girls as we walked through the heavy doors and then down the drive towards the gates. When I looked back I saw Sister and the other staff were waving and so I waved back.

Again I looked back and they were still waving.

I had a moment to look back at the hospital with its mullioned windows, its little towers, one with a flag-pole set upon it. I looked at the dining-room windows, the wire mesh facade of Fortitude Ward and then the French windows of Patience Ward, where Christine had spent her last hours.

As we walked further down the street I looked back and Sister was still waving, but alone now.

I kept looking back, waving to the lone figure in the doorway, and she was still waving.

I waved back in tears until she was completely out of sight.

Epilogue.

In 1964 I felt a great need to see Sister Devereaux again, so my husband and I, together with our two young sons, visited the hospital where she was still working as a Sister.

The young woman I remembered was now aged around fifty but looked very much older. She was still slender, but the passing of time had dimmed the sparkle in her eyes and her hair was turning grey. She kissed and hugged me and shook hands with my husband and was delighted with my children, taking my youngest son, Stuart, in her arms.

Unfortunately only I who was allowed to tour the hospital due to an outbreak of chicken pox (to which only I was immune).

We walked hand in hand and not once did she let go.

The tour was a disappointment in one respect because I hardly recognised the place. Not one room remained the same or had the same function. Fortitude Ward was gone completely. The wall of netting had been bricked up and the corridor wall also demolished and had become a part of a self-service cafeteria. Not a trace of the smell of carbolic remained.

A large number of children, who were dressed in their own clothes, not uniforms, surrounded me. They were running around and making lots of noise, yet not once did Sister quieten them.

I could not stay as long as I would have liked, for I was conscious of my husband and children waiting in the car. It was an emotional goodbye for both of us. But for me I knew I owed my present health and happiness to her care, all those years ago.

In 1969 Sister Devereaux had to take early retirement due to ill health. I corresponded with her for many years until her until her death in the early 1970's.

Her letters always began with '*Dear Forget-Me-Not*' and ended: '*With sincere love.*'

245

Printed in Great Britain
by Amazon

28011107R00139